Medicare Survival Guide®
ADVANCED

The Basic Parts A, B, C & D
and Beyond

A Non-Governmental Resource

Medicare Survival Guide®
ADVANCED

The Basic Parts A, B, C & D
and Beyond

A Non-Governmental Resource

Toni King

REGNERY
CAPITAL
Washington, D.C.

Cataloging-in-Publication data on file with the Library of Congress

ISBN: 978-1-68451-421-2
eISBN: 978-1-68451-422-9

Medicare Disclaimer: This book is not associated, endorsed, or authorized by the Social Security Administration, the Department of Health and Human Services, or the Centers for Medicare & Medicaid Services. This book contains basic information about Medicare, services related to Medicare, and services for Medicare beneficiaries. If you would like more information about the federal government's Medicare program, please visit the office U.S. Government's site for Medicare beneficiaries located at www.medicare.gov.

Disclaimer Limit of Liability/Disclaimer of Warranty: The publisher and author make no representations or warranties with respect to the accuracy or completeness of this guide and specifically disclaim all warranties, including without limitation warranties for a specific purpose. No warranty may be created or extended by sales or promotional materials. The advice and strategies contained herein may not be suitable for every situation. This work is sold with the understanding that the publisher or author is not engaged in giving legal, financial, medical, or insurance advice or other professional services. If professional assistance is required, the services of a competent professional person should be sought. Neither the publisher nor the author shall be liable for damages arising here from. The fact that an organization or website is referred to in this book as a citation and/or a potential source of further information does not mean that the author or the publisher endorses the information the organization or website may provide or recommendations it may make. Readers should be aware that internet websites listed in this book may have changed or disappeared between when this book is written and/or read.

Published in the United States by
Regnery Capital, an Imprint of
Regnery Publishing
A Division of Salem Media Group
Washington, D.C.
www.Regnery.com

Manufactured in the United States of America

10 9 8 7 6 5 4 3 2 1

Dedication

I want to extend a special Thanks to the local editors of each Houston Chronicle/ Houston Community weekly neighborhood throw newspaper which gave me the platform to write the Toni Says® Medicare Column.

Most of all I want to thank God for putting the passion in my heart to not give up and to fight each day helping those that do not understand this complicated governmental system and need guidance and assistance in making their correct Medicare choices.

Many Blessings,

Toni King

Contents

Toni's Medicare Journey

On October 10, 2010, I began my journey as a weekly Medicare columnist in 3 of the Houston Community Newspapers, the Fort Bend Sun, Sugar Land Sun and Katy Rancher. I never dreamed that I would become the local Medicare expert in the Houston Texas are

Now 10 years later, the Toni Says® Medicare column is in most of the Houston Chronicle weekly newspapers (that purchased the HCN newspapers in 2016) totally about 31 various Houston metro and surrounding cities.

Each week, many of the Toni Says® weekly readers visit the Toni Says® office with folders of the weekly articles cut out and saved for future use because they cannot receive an adequate answer from the Medicare and You Handbook or when they call Medicare or Social Security 800 number asking their specific questions.

It was then, that I decided to take the weekly articles and expand my original Medicare Survival Guide® book because the average American's Medicare needs have changed. Baby Boomers who are retiring with or without company benefits are confused and overwhelmed due to companies changing or stopping retiree Medicare benefits. They all want and need answers to their specific needs.

The motto at the Toni Says® office is,
with "Medicare, It's what You DON'T Know that WILL hurt you!!"

Take your time viewing the different sections and topics such as "Enrolling in Medicare at the Right Time or the Right Way?", "Different Medicare Plans" and "Understanding the Famous Donut Hole". If your situation is not found in this guide, then email the Toni Says® website with your questions and one of the Toni Says® team will respond. We can be reached at **info@tonisays.com** or visit my website at **www.Tonisays.com**.

Happy Medicare Search,

Many Blessings,

Toni

“To Do” List for People New to Medicare

Make sure you get your “Welcome Kit” from Medicare at least 3-4 months prior to turning 65 or, if under 65, it will come when you are approved for Medicare, or past 65 when enrolling in Medicare after retiring leaving employer benefits.

Make sure you have Medicare “Part B” *(Medical care)* on your Medicare red, white and blue card. Original Medicare has 2 parts. Part A for Hospital which is free but Part B for Medical *(doctor's services out-patient care and services, home health care, etc.)* you must enroll in Part B and pay a premium to have all the benefits that Part B covers

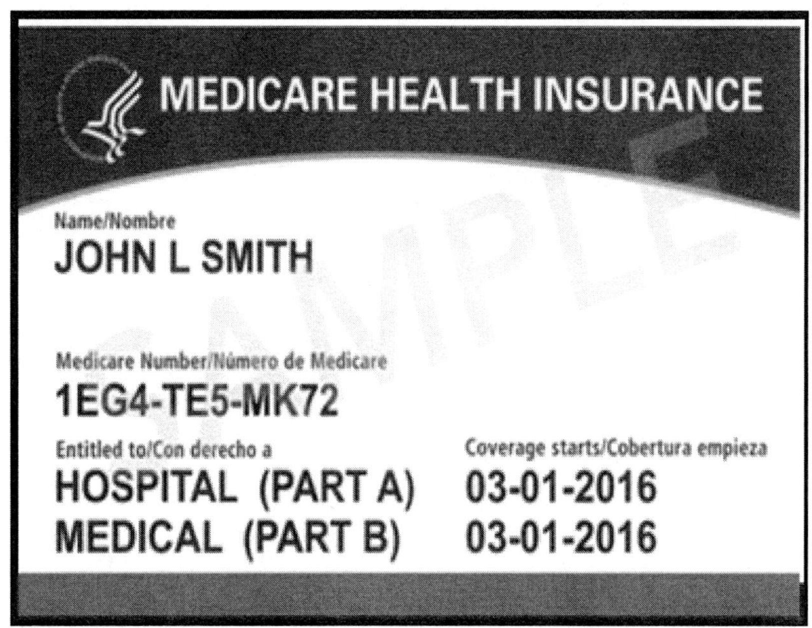

If you have insurance from an employer, union, VA, or TRICARE, check with Human Resources to see how the plan works with Medicare "Part B". **VERY IMPORTANT**

Get a **"Welcome to Medicare"** physical exam within your first 6 months of having Medicare Part B. *(Don't be fooled. This is not a free physical. Co-pays and Part B deductible will apply.)*

Ask your Doctor which preventive services (*like screenings, shots, and tests*) you should get. Bring your list and get **medical** check list online at https://www.medicare.gov/Pubs/pdf/10110.pdf then take to your doctor to schedule the preventative services.

Important Web Sites and Phone Numbers

MEDICARE – www.medicare.gov

1/800-MEDICARE 800/633-4227 TTY users **877/486-2048**

SOCIAL SECURITY – www.socialsecurity.gov

To Enroll in Medicare www.socialsecurity.gov/medicareonly

Social Security Account www.socialsecurity.gov/myaccount

/800-772-1213 TTY users 1/800-325-0778

Call for address or name changes, death notification, to enroll in Medicare, to replace your Medicare card, to get information about signing up for EXTRA HELP with prescription drug costs, and about Social Security Benefits.

RAILROAD RETIREMENT BOARD

Local RRB office or 1/877-772-5772

Call for address or name changes, death notification, to enroll in Medicare and to replace your card.

MEDICAID - Contact your local Medicaid office

The History of Medicare

The person, who is on Medicare today, is no different than those on Medicare when LBJ signed Medicare into law on July 30, 1965. Little did President Johnson know just how confusing the new government program would be for the average individual on Medicare? I bet you cannot imagine what the first premium for Part B of Medicare was in 1965. Are you sitting down? It was a whopping $3.00 a month

As President Johnson signed Medicare into law, former President Truman was sitting beside him to see his idea happen. President Truman lobbied for years to get a program that would help those receiving Social Security benefits. He knew that the average person that was on social security could not afford their health care. What would President Truman think about today's health care situation?

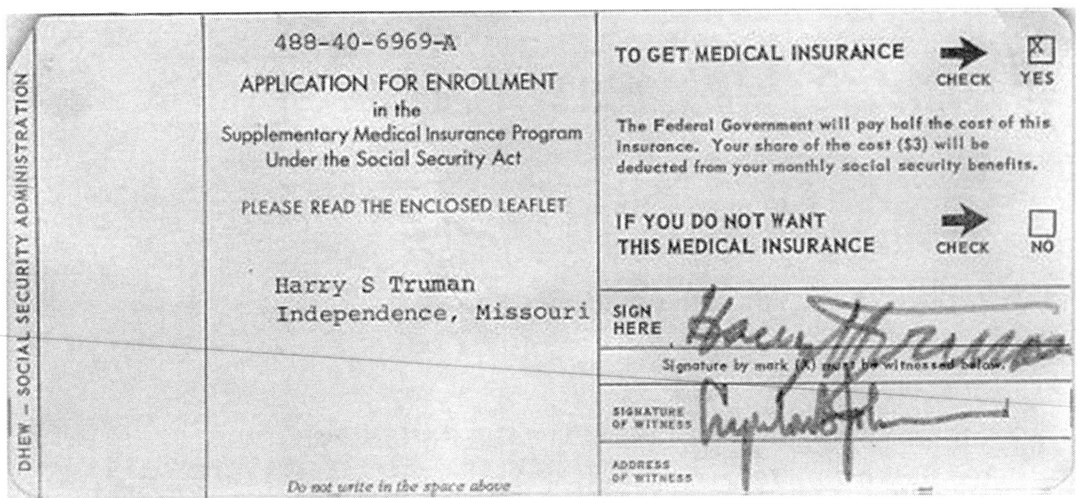
DHEW – SOCIAL SECURITY ADMINISTRATION

488-40-6969-A

APPLICATION FOR ENROLLMENT
in the
Supplementary Medical Insurance Program
Under the Social Security Act

PLEASE READ THE ENCLOSED LEAFLET

Harry S Truman
Independence, Missouri

Do not write in the space above

TO GET MEDICAL INSURANCE → CHECK [X] YES

The Federal Government will pay half the cost of this insurance. Your share of the cost ($3) will be deducted from your monthly social security benefits.

IF YOU DO NOT WANT THIS MEDICAL INSURANCE → CHECK [ ] NO

SIGN HERE

Signature by mark (X) must be witnessed below.

SIGNATURE OF WITNESS

ADDRESS OF WITNESS

President Truman was the first person to enroll in the Medicare Program. I wonder if Mr. Truman would be as confused as most people on Medicare about understanding the rules that Medicare has, or if he would even know how to stay out of the famous “Donut Hole”?

Medicare has its problems, but it is still here for you! The first Part B premium was $3.00 a month. In 2000, the Part B premium was $45.40 per month and in January 2022; the Part B premium is $170.10.

In today’s times, a Medicare beneficiary’s Part B premium is income based depending on what your MAGI (modified adjusted gross income) is. Below are the Medicare Part B and Part D prescription drug IRMAA (income related monthly adjusted amount) premiums. Below are the 2022 Medicare Part B and Part D premiums.

Part B (Medical Insurance) Monthly Premium

(Example Only)

(Monthly Premiums Change Each Year)

If your Yearly Income is File Individual Tax Return	If your Yearly Income is File Joint Tax Return	You Pay
$91,000 or Below	$182,000 or Below	Your Plan Premium
$91,000.01-$114,000	$182,000.01-$228,000	$12.30 + Your Plan Premium
$114,00.01-$142,000	$228,000.01-$284,000	$32.80 + Your Plan Premium
$142,000.01-$170,000	$284,000.01-$340,000	$51.70 + Your Plan Premium
$170,000.01-500,000	$340,000.01-$750,000	$71.30 + Your Plan Premium
Above $500,000.01	Above 750,000.01	$77.90 + Your Plan Premium

Part C (Medicare Advantage Plan) and
Part D (Medicare Prescription Drug) Monthly Premium

(Example Only)

(Monthly Premiums Change Each Year)

Part D (Medicare Prescription Drug) Monthly Premium

If your Yearly Income is File Individual Tax Return	If your Yearly Income is File Joint Tax Return	You Pay
$91,000 or Below	$182,000 or Below	Your Plan Premium
$91,000.01-$114,000	$182,000.01-$228,000	$12.30 + Your Plan Premium
$114,00.01-$142,000	$228,000.01-$284,000	$32.80 + Your Plan Premium
$142,000.01-$170,000	$284,000.01-$340,000	$51.70 + Your Plan Premium
$170,000.01-500,000	$340,000.01-$750,000	$71.30 + Your Plan Premium
Above $500,000.01	Above 750,000.01	$77.90 + Your Plan Premium

Every year, Part B and Part D premiums rise with the Medicare deductibles increasing, but the benefits stay the same. How much more can your social security check handle and will there be any money left for you to spend the way you want? You're surprised and frustrated that your social security check does not cover your expenses for the entire month. "There seems to be more month left than the money you have. Your money will only stretch so far!!"

Chapter 1
Enrolling in Medicare the Right Way

With 10,000 Baby Boomers turning 65 every day for the next 18 years, enrolling in Medicare can become increasingly confusing. Most believe that when they turn 65, a magical switch turns on and poof, you are automatically on Medicare! Unfortunately, Medicare has enrollment rules that must be adhered to

Most think that Medicare begins the day of your 65th birthday, when actually Medicare begins the t day of the month that you turn 65, for example if your birthday is March 16 (or any date in March), then your Medicare will begin March 1 t not the date of your birthday, in this example March 16th If your birthday is the 1 t of March, then your Medicare will begin February 1 t... the first day of the prior month.

You would think that Medicare would enroll you in Medicare. Medicare does not know how to enroll you in Medicare because the Social Security Office processes the paperwork. The lines at the local Social Security offices are astronomically long. In today's internet times, the Social Security Administration wants you to enroll, online at the Social Security website www.socialsecurity.gov/benefits/medicare Doing this online saves a lot of time and frustration.

Social Security will begin enrolling you in Medicare at least 90 days prior to turning 65. If you wait until the month that you turn 65, then your Medicare will begin the next month

Toni Says® *Don't wait until the last minute to enroll in Medicare because if you have not enrolled in Medicare, then you do not have the benefits that Medicare offers*

Please read the additional information in this chapter about your specific enrollment situation and the different way to enroll such as:

1) Are you turning 65 and receiving your Social Security check? Different way to enroll.
2) Are you turning 65, receiving your Social Security check and enrolled in your spouse's (who is working full-time) company group health benefits? Different way to enroll
3) Are you turning 65, not receiving your Social Security check, not working full-time with company benefits? Different way to enroll.
4) Are you turning 65, not receiving your Social Security check, working full-time with no company benefits, maybe an individual plan or VA benefits? Different way to enroll.
5) Are you turning 65, not receiving your Social Security check, working full-time with company benefits? Different way to enroll.
6) Are you turning 65, not working full-time or retired and have health benefits or retirement benefits from either your past employer or your spouse's employer? Different way to enroll.
7) Are you past 65, retiring from your current employment and never enrolled in Medicare Parts A and/or B?

Search through the table of contents for your specific Medicare enrollment situation or read the rest of this chapter and gain Medicare enrollment knowledge to help your friends that are confused.

Below are articles from the Toni Says® newspaper column regarding specific questions regarding enrolling in Medicare. Each article is a true situation, we have changed the names to protect the individuals.

How to Enroll in Medicare at the Right Time!!

Hello Toni:

I am turning 65 in December and have not started receiving my Social Security check. I am still working full time but do not have company benefits. I'm confused because I do not have Social Security and not sure how to get my Medicare. Do I call Medicare or what to enroll? Do I have to be receiving my Social Security check to get Medicare? Can you please explain what I should do?

Thanks, John, Longview, TX

Hi there, John:

Enrolling in Medicare can be very confusing! Most people think that when they turn 65, a magical switch is turned on and poof you are on Medicare! Medicare changed the rules during the Clinton administration, when Social Security extended the time for receiving 100% of your social security benefits

To receive your Medicare card on time depends on whether you are receiving your social security check. Receiving your social security check is your ticket to Medicare. It starts the process for you to receive your Medicare benefits and your Medicare card.

Social Security does all of the paperwork for Medicare and now with healthcare reform Social Security has changed how they want you to enroll. Social Security wants you to enroll in Medicare online at **socialsecurity.gov/benefits/medicare**. The wait is over 3 hours at many local Social Security office , so doing this on-line saves you a lot of time and frustration.

How to receive your Medicare at the right time:

- **Turning 65 and Receiving Your Social Security Check** is the easiest way to receive your card. Medicare will send your "Welcome to Medicare" kit **90 days** before you turn 65 with your Medicare card in the kit. If you do not receive it, then go to Social Security and find out where your card is! Remember, Social Security processes all the paperwork for Medicare
- **Turning 65 and NOT Receiving a Social Security Check** - because you are still working or may not be working, but waiting past 65 to receive 100% of your Social Security. Contact Social Security **90** days before you turn 65. It takes Social Security **90** days to do the paperwork and if you wait until you have turned 65, then you will only have Medicare Part A benefits and no benefits of what "Part B" covers. Social Security takes **90** days to the paperwork for Medicare. Always check with Human Resources if you are delaying "Part B". Many health insurance carriers are changing their rules regarding "Part B" and may require you to enroll in Medicare
- **Turning 65 and still working"**- Talk to your Employer's Human Resources. Ask if you need to enroll in Part B. If you do not need Part B because you are "still working" or your spouse is "still working" and you may be on their group plan, then call Social Security to delay "Part B" and let them know that you have creditable coverage with your group plan. You will receive your

Medicare card with "Part A Hospital Only". See the Medicare and You Handbook about delaying Part B or call Toni and visit with her or anyone on our team that can assist in your Medicare needs.

- **Under 65 and Receiving Social Security Disability** will receive their Medicare automatically on their 25th month of receiving their disability check. Make sure that you have applied for both Medicare's Part A and B

 **Toni Says®** Take your time when enrolling in Medicare. Know your Medicare options.

Medicare Initial Enrollment Period for Turning 65

						Birthday					
						Enrollment Peroid					
Jan	Feb	Mar	Apr 1	May 2	June 3	July Birthday	Aug 5	Sept 6	Oct 7	Nov	Dec
		If you join during:	Three months BEFORE			Month of	Three Months AFTER			Missed Enrollment Peroid	

How to Apply for Medicare Online when turning 65 Avoiding Long Lines at Your Local Social Security Office!!

Hi Toni

I am turning 65 and I was surprised when Social Security told me to go online to sign up. They did not want me to go to the Social Security office to sign up and that I now need to start a "My Social Security Account" to begin the process.

I am concerned that if I go online, I will have to begin receiving my Social Security check. I retired in 2018 and want to not begin my Social Security check until I am 70

Can you please explain in simple terms where to go online, so that I can enroll in Medicare the right way? Thanks in advance,

Carla from Arizona

Carla

With budget problems, Social Security discovered 2 years ago how much payroll or should I say "our" tax dollars could be saved by finally going online to have people file for their Medicare cards when they were turning 65 and not receiving their Social Security check.

Unless you are receiving your Social Security check at least 90 days prior to turning 65, then Medicare has no idea that you are turning 65 and should be receiving your Medicare card with Parts A and/or B because Social Security doesn't know that you are turning 65. Social Security processes all Medicare applications for Medicare. Medicare does not enroll their own applications.

Carla, you mentioned that you are not receiving your Social Security check, not working full time with true company benefits and that Social Security advised you to enroll online. The best timeline is 90 days prior to turning 65 to the month prior to your 65th birthday and you should visit **www.ssa.gov/benefits/medicare** to enroll for Medicare to begin the 1 t day of the month you turn 65.

When you begin the process of enrolling in Medicare, Social Security will ask if you have a have a "My Social Security account".

If you do have a "My Social Security account":

- please have your user name and password handy to begin your Medicare enrollment in Parts A and/or B application.

If you don't have a "My Social Security Account":

- Carla starting a "My Social Security Account" does not begin your Social Security check.
- Please register yourself and your spouse now for a "My Social Security Account" months before applying for Medicare to be prepared when you are ready to apply when turning 65 and need to apply for both Medicare Parts A and/or B with an account by visiting www.ssa.gov/myaccount.
- You should know your credit history because Social Security will pull credit information from your credit history to verify that this information is unique to only your and/or your spouse's credit file. Don't worry this confuses many.

Let's discuss how to apply online and a few of the problems we are discovering when helping others apply for Medicare online when turning 65 by going online to www.ssa.gov/benefits/medicare._What if you cannot open a "My Social Security Account", then what? Click on the **EXIT** button and proceed to the Medicare sign up page. This information cannot be found anywhere on any Social Security information on "How to Enroll in Medicare". If you cannot proceed with applying for Medicare without opening a "My Social Security Account" than what? Go directly to your local Social Security office and inform the Social Security agent that you are not able to open a Social Security account and are locked out and you need help.

Information to apply only for Medicare is below:

1) Begin with your information: Name, Social Security number, Gender and Date of Birth
2) Contact information with address, phone number, email address
3) Citizen information about you with what language your read and speak
4) Questions about your health benefits
5) Then submit your application online and view your receipt which explains what additional information may be needed such as marriage license when you are short of 40 quarters and applying under your spouse's Medicare benefits or may be like Norman and must take your citizenship papers. Take this information to the local Social Security office to be verified.
6) Once your beneficiary verification letter that comes first and includes your Medicare number and Part A and/or B dates, or your new Medicare Card which comes next, then enroll in a Medicare Supplement or Medicare Advantage Plan and Medicare Prescription drug plan.

Medicare Effective Date Schedule

(time to enroll when turning 65 without company benefits)

Situation	When you sign Up	Medicare Begins
With or without Social Security	Auto enroll before 65th birthday	^{t} day of Birth-month unless your birthday is on the 1 ^{t} then it starts the ^{t} of the previous month
With or without Social Security	Your birthday is on the 1 ^{t} day of the month	Starts ^{t} of previous month
	Month you turn 65	1 month after you sign up
	the month after you are 65	2 months after you sign up
	2 months after you are 65	3 months after you sign up
	3 months after you are 65	3 months after you sign up
**After that time	you can only apply during the General Election Period (Jan 1 ^{t} 31 ^{t}) unless you have a SEP (Special Election Period)	Medicare will start on July 1 ^{t}

Special Enrollment Circumstances

I Have Rheumatoid Arthritis and Need Medicare Begin ASAP!

Toni

I have a very different Medicare problem concerning how to enroll in Medicare than any problem I've seen in your column

Currently I have rheumatoid arthritis and my prescriptions are very expensive. I turn 65 on December 20th and need my Medicare to begin January 1st. My husband is retiring and losing his company benefits effective January 1st

I am a non-working spouse and do not have enough quarters to receive Medicare on my own. I don't know how to apply for my husband's benefits. What do I do? Looking forward to your response

Mary Ann, Hempstead, TX

Mary Ann:

It is so very important to plan ahead, when you or the "working" spouse is retiring, then there is no concern that you are enrolling in Medicare correctly. Always begin at least 90 days prior to you turning 65 or beginning your Medicare Part B to start enrolling in Medicare. Many wait until the month they are receiving Medicare as you have and sometimes that can be too late

Mary Ann, when you are speaking to Social Security about applying for Medicare; ask how you can apply under your husband's Social Security number, because you are short the 40 quarters to qualify under your own Social Security number. They will schedule an appointment either over the phone or at a local Social Security office and will advise how to apply under your husband's work record. You will need an "original" certified marriage license to verify that you are currently married

Medicare has what is called **the enrollment effective date schedule**, which is not mentioned in the Medicare and You Handbook. The handbook, under "Initial Enrollment Period", states, "If you enroll in Part A and/or Part B the month you turn 65 or during the last 3 months of your Initial Enrollment Period, the start date for your Medicare coverage will be delayed".

The **"effective date schedule"** is the 7-month period which occurs 3 months before turning 65, the month you turn 65 and 3 months after turning 65, but it is not as simple as this.

Below is the Medicare effective date schedule

- Enrolling anytime 3 months before turning 65, your Medicare begins the first day of the month you turn 65.

Since you, Mary Ann will turn 65 on December 20, you could have enrolled in Medicare Part A and/or B in September, October, or November (3 months prior) for a December 1st effective date

- Enroll the month you turn 65, then Medicare will begin 1 month after you sign up.

Mary Ann, you can enroll in December; and your Medicare will begin January 1st

- Enroll 1 month after you turn 65, your Medicare will begin **2 months** after you sign up.

If Mary Ann enrolls in January; her Medicare begins March 1st

- Enroll 2 months after you turn 65, your Medicare will begin **3 months** after you sign up.

Had Mary Ann enrolled in February; her Medicare will begin May1st

- Enroll 3 months after you turn 65, your Medicare will begin **3 months** after you sign up.

Had Mary Ann enrolled in March (3 months after the month you turn 65); her Medicare will begin June 1st (3 months later)

Mary Ann, since you want your Medicare to begin January 1st, I would advise you to contact Social Security ASAP because you need your effective date to begin in a few weeks

Married VS Domestic Partner, Turning 65 and Delaying Medicare Part B…not a good option!

Toni

Your name was given to my husband by the person who cleans our pool and religiously reads your column in his local newspaper

My problem is different than most couples because now I am finding out that my company's group health plan is not paying for ***any*** *Medicare Part B medical expenses because my husband is really a domestic partner. We have been together for over 25 years, but never officially married. Richard is 72 and I am a 58-year-old female who now needs to learn the maze of Medicare*

Richard has serious health issues with 2 stents in his heart and a recent back surgery, which is now costing us thousands of dollars because my company's group health plan is not paying for his doctor's care. Richard has never enrolled in Medicare Part B because I have always been the "working spouse". Now I am discovering that the Cigna group health plan (the company's self-administered group health plan) does not recognize "domestic partners" as a married couple because we do not have a marriage license

Now, he needs to enroll in Medicare Part B, and with him being 72 if he doesn't do this correctly the penalty will be over 7 years. From what I have read in your articles, that this could be 70 or 80% penalty, forever. The bottom line is, We need HELP!!

Thank You Gabby from the Katy, TX

Gabby, you are in the middle of the maze of Medicare!

This needs to be a rush job! Richard needs Medicare Part B immediately!

This is a new question that I had never thought about and everyone needs to know the rules of Medicare regarding delaying Medicare Part B, when there is an unmarried domestic partner situation (same sex or opposite sex) and they receive health insurance through their partner's employer.

Always discuss delaying your domestic partner's Medicare Part B with your company's health insurance benefits administrator or HR department about what is in the insurance company's handbook regarding unmarried domestic spouse Medicare rules.

The size of the group makes a difference. When there are under 100 employees on your unmarried spouse's group health insurance plan, you should generally not delay the non-working domestic partner or common law spouse's Part B. When there are over 100 employees, then consult your benefits or HR department about if your domestic partner can delay their Medicare Part B, without receiving a late penalty, when they need to enroll in Medicare Part B at a later date

I have written about the "**Special Enrollment Period**" and having the Social Security form titled "Request for Employment Information" filled out by your HR or office manager. This must be done ASAP, and Richard could have his Medicare Part B with an effective date of September 1, but Richard will have to take the form down to your local Social Security office, meet with a Social Security agent in person and always get copies of everything the Social Security Agent says and/or signs you up for.

Toni Says® Meet with a Social Security Agent and give them the form, DO NOT mail it to Social Security or put it in the drop box! There are **no do-overs** with Medicare or Social Security!

Self Employed…Not Enrolling in
Part B Causes a Medicare Nightmare

Good Day, Toni:

We saw your answer about Medicare Part B nightmare in an article online and our situation is different. My wife and I are turning 65, me this February 8th and Carol April 12th. We have signed up for Medicare Part A only

I retired 2 years ago with fantastic retiree benefits for both of us. Currently, I am self-employed and paid as a 1099 contract worker, but I do not have health benefits from that company

We do not see a need to sign up for Medicare Part B because we are covered under an existing employer retiree plan. Are we correct in this assumption of not enrolling in Part B? Neither the HR department nor Medicare can give us a straight answer

When do you advise us to sign up for Part B?

Thanks, Richard and Carol from Alexander, VA

Hello Richard and Carol

Great Medicare question I would advise you to enroll in Part B **NOW**!! Don't wait because your enrollment time is running out.

Recently, the Toni Says® office consulted with a person that is also self-employed, but given wrong advice from a well-meaning friend about delaying his Part B. His Medicare nightmare is now starting, which is what you and Carol might have if you do not enroll the correct way.

Medicare recognizes true company and union health plans with the Medicare recipient **working full time for that company** for one to delay Part B for the working and non-working spouse

The Medicare and You Handbook says, "COBRA and retiree health coverage **do not** count as **current employer coverage**". Individual and retirement health plans **are not current employer coverage** for those that are self-employed as you are or retired

The self-employed person that I consulted with is now 66 and will receive a 10% penalty for each 12-month period which you could have had Part B but failed to enroll. His penalty will be 20% penalty (2 years 65 and 66) each month for as long as he is on Medicare. The 20% penalty will increase as the Part B premium increases.

Right now, is your Medicare "Initial Enrollment Period" which is a 7-month period that begins when you turn 65. You and your wife have 3 months before turning 65, the month you turn 65 and 3 months after to enroll in Parts A and B keeping from receiving the Part B 10% penalty for each 12-month period which you could have had Part B, but failed to enroll.

I advise anyone who contacts me for Medicare consultation to enroll in Medicare Parts A and B when you are **"not working fulltime" for a company**. Not working full time with true company benefits is what Medicare looks for to keep from giving you the 10% Part B penalty.

Enroll in Medicare the correct way when you are turning 65 or after 65 retiring from your company because you do not get a second chance. "I didn't know" is not a good excuse for Medicare or Social Security that processes the paperwork for Medicare!

Toni Says® Whether self-employed or enrolled in an individual health plan be sure to enroll in both Medicare Parts A and B when one does not have a working sp

Should Veterans Using the VA enroll in Medicare Part B?

Dear Toni

I am a Viet Nam Vet, turning 65, and recently I was at the VA when someone told me that if I use the VA for my Medicare benefits that I don't have to enroll in Medicare.)

My wife reads your column and informed me that I will get a penalty if I enroll later. I don't want to lose my VA benefit, but I don't want to have money taken out of my Social Security check for Medicare Part B, if I don't have to. You are the expert, what is my best choice?

Jim from Beaumont, TX

Oh Jim

I am to glad hear that your wife reads my column, because she has saved you tons of Medicare stress. Enrolling in original Medicare which is Parts A and B will not cause you to lose your VA medical benefits. In fact, enrolling in Medicare helps you if you need medical benefits outside of the VA

For a person to qualify for Medicare you must have worked and paid Social Security and Medicare taxes from your payroll check? The protentional Medicare Beneficiary must have worked only 10 years or 40 quarters (paying taxes), to qualify for Medicare Part A, at no additional cost. When you sign up for Medicare Part A, you will also need to enroll in Part B, which has a monthly premium.

I would advise you and any Veteran reading this article to enroll in Medicare Parts A and B. In fact, the VA encourages Veterans to enroll in Part B.

I am very well aware that you do not need "Part B" to receive medical care from the VA, but if you ever go outside of the VA for any medical treatment (and you want Medicare to help pick up some of the cost) you do need Part B. You might be ambulanced to another hospital that is not a VA facility for a medical emergency, or you may go to MD Anderson for cancer treatment, then **you will pay 100% of the medical charges that "Part B"** covers, because you do not have Part B.

Part B covers all your outpatient needs, doctor services such as office visits and even surgery, MRIs, CT Scans, chemotherapy, and the list can go on. Without Part B of Medicare, a person might have to pay 100% out their pocket for services associated with Part B and this could be in the $1,000s or hundreds of thousands of dollars

Chemotherapy, usually done on an outpatient basis, falls under Medicare Part B. I don't know how much chemotherapy is, but if you are not enrolled in Part B, you will pay 100% for the chemo if it is not received at the VA. I wouldn't want you or any other Veteran take the chance because someone at the VA, who had no earthly idea what they were talking about, were giving **incorrect advice**

Many who do not enroll in Part B when they are first eligible for Medicare, may have to pay a "late enrollment" penalty of 10% for each full 12-month period that they could have had Part B, but did not sign up for it.

Let's says you waited 50 months, which is a 4 full 12-month period, then the Part B penalty is an additional 40% (4 years x 10%+40%) added to the current Part B premium, for as long as you have Medicare

Not enrolling in Part D (Medicare Prescription Drug plan) is another story. Medicare considers the VA credible coverage and when you enroll in Part D, at a later date, you do not get the late enrollment penalty. Guess what, the VA prescription drug coverage has no Part D donut hole!

Husband Laid Off ... Will Medicare Pay for Medical Care Overseas as a Contract Worker When He Turns 65

Toni

My husband, who is turning 65 this September, was laid off from a major oil company this year and the only way he can make a living is, as an engineer on a contract basis employee with no benefits. I am a stay at home wife, who is now on COBRA

My question for you is, whether he should apply for Medicare and since he will live outside of the United States, can he receive Medicare coverage in the various oil related countries overseas where he will be living and traveling on a daily basis? How does Medicare pay if he is receiving care while he is working overseas?

By the way, he is living in Saudi Arabia and I will have to email him your answers

Thanks, Angela from Cy Fair

Hello Angela:

Yes, your husband should enroll in Medicare because he is not working full time with "true" company benefits. Medicare will **NOT** pay for any medical care while one is overseas. I will discuss what your husband should do while working overseas and get medical care later in this article

The first thing your husband needs to know is that because he is turning 65, this September, his time is ticking to have Medicare begin by September 1st when his Medicare Parts A and B can begin. He can go online in August to **www.socialsecurity.gov/benefits/medicare** to enroll in both Medicare Parts A and B

Medicare gives you a 7-month window to enroll before one begins receiving the "famous" Part B penalty. The 7-month window starts 3 months before your turn 65, the month you turn 65 and 3 months after which is called Medicare's Initial Enrollment Period

During a Toni Says® Medicare consultation, the team stresses the unique value of receiving Medicare Part B for the first time, such as when one is turning 65 and/or past 65 and retiring with "true" company benefits

During this unique time, when you are enrolling in a Medicare Supplement/Medigap, such as your husband may want to, he will have a 6 month, Medicare Supplement/Medigap Open Enrollment Period where he will not have to answer any health questions to qualify for the specific Medicare Supplement/ Medigap plan.

Your husband will have Medicare Parts A and B with a Medicare Supplement/Medigap to take care of his medical care while in the United States. Now, he can also enroll in a Medicare Part D prescription drug plan.

He needs to be aware that a Medicare Supplement/Medigap does not have adequate coverage for traveling overseas to foreign countries.

A Medicare Supplement/Medigap provides $50,000 of foreign travel benefit not covered by Medicare with a $250 deductible, where you pay 20% of the $50,000 and the insurance company pays 80% of the $50,000 lifetime benefit.

For your husband to work overseas, he will need to apply for overseas travel insurance to help with any type of medical need he while he is working to care for his family and use his Medicare when he comes back to the states. Angela, you also, will want to have travel insurance if you go to an overseas visit

I Should Not Have Enrolled Medicare Part B while Working with Company Benefits Cost Me $7,500 and Part B Never Paid?

Dear Toni

When I turned 65, friends told me to enroll in Part B to keep from getting the Part B penalty, even though I had great company benefits with the company I had worked for 30+ years. Now, I would like to get a Medicare Supplement, but I am finding out I cannot get any plan I want like my other co-workers, who are way past 65 and are now receiving their Medicare Part B

I would like to get a Medicare Supplement Plan G, but because I've had Part B in place, I can't due of heart surgery I had 2 years ago. Now, I have to answer health questions because my insurance agent says I don't qualify for Medicare Supplement Open enrollment. I've paid $7,500 for Medicare Part B when I could have waited

Please explain what is going on and why Medicare doesn't keep us informed of the rules. I need to get Medicare Supplement coverage for both me and my wife? We need your help

Thanks, George, New Orleans, LA

Hello George:

Every day I talk to someone who gets the wrong information from a well-meaning friend. As for Medicare not educating folks about their rules, please don't get me started on that one. As I have said before, Medicare provides special rules for those who are "still working" with true company benefits

The Medicare and You Handbook, explains how to enroll in Medicare and what to do when leaving your company benefits after 65. In the Medicare and You Handbook it says, "When you sign up for Part B, your Medigap Open Enrollment Period begins."

George, you are past your Medicare Supplement/Medigap Open Enrollment Period. The Medicare and You Handbook also states,

> *"The best time to buy a Medigap policy is during your Medigap Open Enrollment Period. This 6-month period begins on the first day of the month in which you're 65 or older* ***and***

enrolled in Part B. (Some states have additional Open Enrollment Periods.) After this enrollment period, you may not be able to buy a Medigap policy. If you're able to buy one, it may cost more."

This is why enrolling in Part B the correct way, when "still working" full-time with true company benefits is so important. Not only to keep from receiving a Medicare Part B penalty, but also to be able to enroll and be accepted in any Medicare Supplement/Medigap plan.

Your saving grace is that you are being terminated from you or your spouse's company benefits and can receive a 63-day guaranteed issue period for applying for a Medicare Supplement/Medigap plan. Keep your company benefit termination letter to show the Medicare Supplement insurance company that you are in a guarantee issue period.

With guaranteed issue, an insurance company must:

- Sell you a Medicare Supplement/Medigap policy. "You have the right to buy Medicare Supplement/ Medigap Plan A, B, C, F, K or L that's sold in your state by any insurance company for those with Medicare Part A that begins prior to January 1, 2020. For those who Medicare Part A with Medicare Part B which begins after January 1, 2020, then Medicare Plan G and High-Deductible Plan G will be offered in place of Medicare Supplement Plan C, Plan F and High-Deductible Plan F.
- Cover all your pre-existing health conditions.
  Cannot charge you more for a Medicare Supplement/Medigap policy, regardless of past or present health problems. As stated in the "Choosing a Medigap Policy" by Medicare.

No one realizes the value to first receiving Part B until they are in your situation and now they want to apply for a Medicare Supplement and can only get certain plans because they are no longer in their Medicare Open Enrollment period.

Over 700,000 Receiving Medicare Penalties...

Why?? They Didn't Know the Rules!

Toni

I desperately need your help! I have just discovered that my mother, who is 67, has never enrolled in Medicare Part B or D. She was under the impression that if she didn't go to the doctor, she didn't need to pay the premium because she needs the money to pay for her car payment

She has a huge problem because she has been diagnosed with colon cancer and she does not have Part B or a Medicare prescription drug plan. I called Social Security to help her enroll in Part B and was informed that she has to wait until January 1 thru March 31 of 2017 (next year) to enroll in Medicare Part B because she has missed her "window of opportunity". Can you tell me what I can do to help her?

Thanks, Jeanine from Bellaire, TX

Oh my, Jeanine:

Your mother has an extremely serious Medicare issue because the General Enrollment Period for those that never enrolled in Medicare ended on Thursday, March 31st and as the Social Security rep stated your mother will have to wait until next January 1, to begin her process of enrolling in Medicare Part B. Yes, she will receive a Part B penalty.

She can enroll in Medicare Part D during Medicare Open Enrollment which begins Saturday, October 15 of this year and her new Medicare prescription drug plan will begin January 1, of the following year. She will not be able to enroll in a Medicare Advantage plan because her Medicare Part B will not go into effect until July 1, of next year, if she enrolls during the upcoming General Enrollment Period

When your mother, who will be 68 enrolls in Medicare Part B during Medicare's General Enrollment Period will received a Part B penalty which is a 10% penalty for each 12-month period and for her is 30% (3 years times 10%) for as long as your mother could have had Part B, but failed to enroll. This 30% penalty will never go away and remains in effect for the life of the Medicare beneficiary's Medicare coverage

The Medicare Part B standard premium changes every year. (for year 2017); a beneficiary's premium would increase by 30% as an example for a 3-year penalty for as long as one remains on Medicare Your mother's penalty will be (that year's Part B premium) X (30% penalty) plus the cost of the Part B Premium and this amount changes as Part B premium changes.

The Medicare Part D penalty for is 1% of national Part D average premium and this also changes each year for each month you could have enroll in Part D from age 65, but failed to enroll. Her Part D penalty will be that specific Part D 1% penalty x 36 months, for an extra monthly penalty cost and this amount changes as Part D's premium and monthly penalty changes.

Currently, there are over 700,000 Medicare beneficiaries who are receiving a Medicare Part B and/ or D penalty costing on average $5,000 in Medicare lifetime penalties because they did not enroll under Medicare enrollment periods.

Medicare enrollment periods are listed below:

> **Medicare Initial Enrollment Period**: Begins 3 months before turning 65, the month one turns 65 and 3 months after one turns 65
> **Special Enrollment Period**: Enroll after 65 when delaying Medicare Part B due to working full time with company benefits. This is an 8-month window of signing up for Part B without receiving a Part B penalty.
> **General Enrollment Period**: January 1-March 31 when one who has not enrolled in Part B and now can enroll in Medicare Part B, but **WILL** receive a Part B penalty.

Toni Says® Many believe that they do not need to enroll in Medicare when they are healthy and do not need a doctor. They are not aware of the Medicare Part B and Part D monthly penalty or No Part B or Part D coverage and you will pay 100% for those benefits.

Special Enrollment Period-Rule & Forms

For those leaving their or their spouse's employment benefits past 65…should be followed exactly as Social Security deems. (Remember Social Security enrolls in Medicare even when past 65.)

You or your spouse are **"still working"** are magic words when it comes to enrolling past 65 and losing your or your spouse's company benefits. The Medicare and You Handbook, discusses under the title of "Should I enroll in Part B" about delaying Medicare Part B when you are leaving your or your spouse's group benefits and "that you can sign up for Part B anytime during the 8-month period that begins the month after the employment ends or the coverage ends, whichever happens first".

When we perform a Medicare planning consultation at the Toni Says® office, whether just laid off or retiring, we stress the value of getting Part B for the first time and that Medicare Part B needs to be enrolled in prior to either enrolling in COBRA or retirement group benefits because of continuation of coverage rules that wants to coordinate with Medicare. No Medicare Parts A or B and you have 8 months to enroll without receiving the famous Medicare Part B penalty.

The process to enroll in Medicare Part B, if you have delayed it is as follows

- There are 2 forms available from Social Security's website or you can ask for them from the Toni Says® office. (toni@tonisays.com) On the top of each form write in ***red letters "Special Enrollment Period".*** This tells the Social Security agent that is processing them, you are signing up at the right time and keeps from giving you a penalty. You are applying for a **SEP (Special Enrollment Period).**

    . **Form #1 Request for Employment Information:** proof of group health care coverage based on current employment. If you have had 2 or more jobs since turning 65, then all companies you or your spouse have worked for from age 65 to the time you or your spouse are retiring, to sign this form. If you are married, you will need the same number of forms filled out for your non-working spouse and signed by the companies HR departments for which you or your spouse has worked, proving the non-working spouse was covered by company insurance (if the non-working spouse is Medicare or Medicare eligible) On the top of each form write in ***red letters "Special Enrollment Period".***

Below is a Sample of what the form looks like.

Special Enrollment Period

DEPARTMENT OF HEALTH AND HUMAN SERVICES
CENTERS FOR MEDICARE & MEDICAID SERVICES

Form Approved
OMB No. 0938-0787

REQUEST FOR EMPLOYMENT INFORMATION

SECTION A: To be completed by individual signing up for Medicare Part B (Medical Insurance)

1. Employer's Name
2. Date __/__/____
3. Employer's Address

City — State — Zip Code

4. Applicant's Name
5. Applicant's Social Security Number ___-__-____
6. Employee's Name
7. Employee's Social Security Number ___-__-____

SECTION B: To be completed by Employers

For Employer Group Health Plans ONLY:

1. Is (or was) the applicant covered under an employer group health plan? ☐ Yes ☐ No
2. If yes, give the date the applicant's coverage began. (mm/yyyy) __/____
3. Has the coverage ended? ☐ Yes ☐ No
4. If yes, give the date the coverage ended. (mm/yyyy) __/____
5. When did the employee work for your company?
   From: (mm/yyyy) __/____ To: (mm/yyyy) __/____ Still Employed: (mm/yyyy) __/____
6. If you're a large group health plan and the applicant is disabled, please list the timeframe (all months) that your group health plan was primary payer.
   From: (mm/yyyy) __/____ To: (mm/yyyy) __/____

For Hours Bank Arrangements ONLY:

1. Is (or was) the applicant covered under an Hours Bank Arrangement? ☐ Yes ☐ No
2. If yes, does the applicant have hours remaining in reserve? ☐ Yes ☐ No
3. Date reserve hours ended or will be used? (mm/yyyy) __/____

All Employers:

2 **Form #2 Application for Enrollment in Medicare** *(a sample copy is below and again in the Forms section)* this is you and your spouse's application for medical insurance from Medicare known as Part B. Social Security fills out this form. Also on the top of each form write in ***red letters "Special Enrollment Period"***

Below is a Sample of what the form looks like.

DEPARTMENT OF HEALTH AND HUMAN SERVICES
CENTERS FOR MEDICARE & MEDICAID SERVICES

Form Approved
OMB No. 0938-1230

APPLICATION FOR ENROLLMENT IN MEDICARE PART B (MEDICAL INSURANCE)

1. Your Social Security Claim Number ☐☐☐-☐☐-☐☐☐☐ Beneficiary Identification Code (BIC) ☐☐☐

2. Do you wish to sign up for Medicare Part B (Medical Insurance)? ☐ YES

3. Your Name (Last Name, First Name, Middle Name)

4. Mailing Address (Number and Street, P.O. Box, or Route)

5. City State ☐☐ Zip Code ☐☐☐☐☐

6. Phone Number (including area code) (☐☐☐) ☐☐☐-☐☐☐☐

7. Written Signature (DO NOT PRINT)
SIGN HERE

8. Date Signed ☐☐/☐☐/☐☐☐☐

IF THIS APPLICATION HAS BEEN SIGNED BY MARK (X), A WITNESS WHO KNOWS THE APPLICANT MUST SUPPLY THE INFORMATION REQUESTED BELOW.

9. Signature of Witness

10. Date Signed ☐☐/☐☐/☐☐☐☐

11. Address of Witness

12. Remarks

Once the form/s is signed by your company HR, take both forms to your local Social Security office for your Medicare to begin when you have retired.

When leaving company benefits, there is an **8-month** window for Medicare Part B enrollment and **63 days** to receive Medicare Prescription Drug Part D plan without receiving a penalty.

The above forms are to be used for all who are asking for a Special Enrollment Period due to leaving company benefits past 65 and want to avoid the famous "Medicare Part B penalty"

SEP form needed - Cancer Treatment Not Covered by Company Insurance...Need to Enroll in Medicare NOW!

Help Toni!

I have developed a rare form of cancer that requires the use of proton therapy at MD Anderson and my problem is that my employer health insurance plan does not cover proton therapy. I will have to pay all of the costs from my 401K

My oncologist's office manager has advised me that because I am over 65, I may want to apply for Medicare Parts A and B. She says that Medicare will pay and provide the care I need

I have seen articles that you write about people leaving their jobs and having to apply for Medicare. I am not leaving or retiring from my job, but I need to begin my Medicare benefits as quickly as possible.

Please advise me what I need to do. David, Houston, TX

David,

During Medicare consultations at the Toni Says® office, we are hearing of various health procedures being excluded from various group health insurance plans and the patient was advised to go to Medicare.

A healthcare professional once told me that many of the newest healthcare and cancer procedures are not readily approved by insurance plans and that these procedures are generally approved with "Original or Traditional Medicare". He said he has to fight the insurance companies every day, to get his patients the care they desperately need.

The process to enroll in Medicare Part A and/or B past 65, is the same whether you or your spouse are leaving company benefits because of:

1) Health issues, since Medicare will pay for the specific procedure you need, that your company benefits will not cover
2) You have been laid off, as so many have in recent months.
3) You have decided to retire.

This procedure must be followed correctly and the step by step process is listed above:

- The forms listed below must be signed by your HR or benefits manager for you and/or your spouse who are covered on company benefits since turning 65.
- There are two forms that Social Security provides from the Social Security website and they are:

  . **Form #1 Request for Employment:** At the top of the form written in red **is "*Special Enrollment Period*"** to inform the Social Security agent that is processing the form that you are signing up at the right time and this should keep you from receiving a Medicare Part B penalty (if your spouse is of Medicare age, they also will need this form filled out by your HR Department and the same "***Special Enrollment Period***" handwritten in Red Ink at the top of the page). This information is needed to process your and/or your spouse's Medicare enrollment application and inform Social Security that you have had company benefits from an employer or employers since age 65. If you have had 2 or more jobs since turning 65, then **each** company you have worked for **<u>must</u>** sign a form (the same for your spouse if they were of Medicare age while they were covered by your company health insurance).

Below is a Sample of what the form looks like.

Special Enrollment Period

DEPARTMENT OF HEALTH AND HUMAN SERVICES
CENTERS FOR MEDICARE & MEDICAID SERVICES

Form Approved
OMB No. 0938-0787

REQUEST FOR EMPLOYMENT INFORMATION

SECTION A: To be completed by individual signing up for Medicare Part B (Medical Insurance)

1. Employer's Name
2. Date ☐☐/☐☐/☐☐☐☐
3. Employer's Address

City | State ☐☐ | Zip Code ☐☐☐☐☐

4. Applicant's Name
5. Applicant's Social Security Number ☐☐☐-☐☐-☐☐☐☐
6. Employee's Name
7. Employee's Social Security Number ☐☐☐-☐☐-☐☐☐☐

SECTION B: To be completed by Employers

For Employer Group Health Plans ONLY:

1. Is (or was) the applicant covered under an employer group health plan? ☐ Yes ☐ No
2. If yes, give the date the applicant's coverage began. (mm/yyyy) ☐☐/☐☐☐☐
3. Has the coverage ended? ☐ Yes ☐ No
4. If yes, give the date the coverage ended. (mm/yyyy) ☐☐/☐☐☐☐
5. When did the employee work for your company?
   From: (mm/yyyy) ☐☐/☐☐☐☐ | To: (mm/yyyy) ☐☐/☐☐☐☐ | Still Employed: (mm/yyyy) ☐☐/☐☐☐☐
6. If you're a large group health plan and the applicant is disabled, please list the timeframe (all months) that your group health plan was primary payer.
   From: (mm/yyyy) ☐☐/☐☐☐☐ | To: (mm/yyyy) ☐☐/☐☐☐☐

2. **Form #2 Application for Enrollment in**: is filled out by Social Security to say when Part B will begin.

Below is a Sample of what the form looks like.

DEPARTMENT OF HEALTH AND HUMAN SERVICES
CENTERS FOR MEDICARE & MEDICAID SERVICES

Form Approved
OMB No. 0938-1230

APPLICATION FOR ENROLLMENT IN MEDICARE PART B (MEDICAL INSURANCE)

1. Your Social Security Claim Number ☐☐☐-☐☐-☐☐☐☐ | Beneficiary Identification Code (BIC) ☐☐☐
2. Do you wish to sign up for Medicare Part B (Medical Insurance)? ☐ YES
3. Your Name (Last Name, First Name, Middle Name)
4. Mailing Address (Number and Street, P.O. Box, or Route)
5. City | State ☐☐ | Zip Code ☐☐☐☐☐
6. Phone Number (including area code) (☐☐☐) ☐☐☐-☐☐☐☐
7. Written Signature (DO NOT PRINT)
   SIGN HERE
8. Date Signed ☐☐/☐☐/☐☐☐☐

IF THIS APPLICATION HAS BEEN SIGNED BY MARK (X), A WITNESS WHO KNOWS THE APPLICANT MUST SUPPLY THE INFORMATION REQUESTED BELOW.

9. Signature of Witness
10. Date Signed ☐☐/☐☐/☐☐☐☐
11. Address of Witness
12. Remarks

Take both forms to your local Social Security office for your Medicare to begin and be sure to make copies of all paperwork given to the Social Security office, just in case the paperwork is lost.

As you can see David, there are options for those who wish to enroll in Medicare that many are not aware exist

Know How to Enroll in Medicare Past 65 and Losing Your Job!!

Toni

I worked for a major oil service company in Fort Bend County and Dec.8th I was part of the 8,000 oil industry employees who were in the lay-offs. I turned 65 in June and only have Medicare Part A and delayed Part B because I have "true" company benefits. Human Resources gave me paperwork regarding applying for retiree Medicare coverage thru a special administrator for my Medicare options

HR said nothing regarding how I should enroll in Medicare's Part B. I've been told from friends that there is a Part B penalty and really want to avoid that disaster. Please advise me what the Medicare Part B enrollment process is. ~

Thanks in Advance, Mike from Sugar Land, TX

Mike

I have been advising more concerned baby boomers on how to enroll in Medicare if one is past 65 and have lost their job, want to be prepared because they may lose their job or want to retire without stress.

Those turning 65 or past 65 should know what paperwork they should have in their desk drawer or briefcase, just in case they get "the pink slip" from the HR department and have HR sign off on the forms before you leave out the door.

If you are married and your spouse is 65 or older and has been on your company insurance you must get a "Request for Employment Information" form for them also and have HR sign it to prove they were on your company Insurance. Just like your form, in RED ink, write across the top of the page "*Special Enrollment Period*", prior to giving or sending the forms to Social Security.

When we perform a Medicare planning consultation at the Toni Says® office whether just laid off or retiring, I always advise them to make sure that they have Part B in place when leaving or losing employment and/or group benefits.

The process to enroll in Part B after you have delayed you Part B is below

1) Call Social Security at 1/800-772-1213 and advise them that you have left your company or are retiring and need to enroll in Part B of Medicare because you had delayed it.
2) You will have a ***Special Enrollment Period*" (SEP)** that last for an 8-month period without receiving a Part B penalty. After the 8-month period that you are no longer working, you will receive a Part B penalty if you enroll in Part B and this penalty goes all the way back to the day you turn 65
3) There are 2 forms that Social Security will send you and on the top of each form hand write in **red letters is *Special Enrollment Period*** for the Social Security agent that is processing them to know that you are signing up at the right time and keep from giving you a penalty. You are applying for a SEP (***Special Enrollment Period***). *(These forms are available at the Toni Says office if you cannot locate them online*
    - **Form #1 Request for Employment Information:** for proof of group health care coverage based on current employment. This information is needed to process your Medicare enrollment application. If you have had 2 or more jobs since turning 65, then each company will have to sign this form.

Below is a Sample of what the form looks like

Special Enrollment Period

DEPARTMENT OF HEALTH AND HUMAN SERVICES
CENTERS FOR MEDICARE & MEDICAID SERVICES

Form Approved
OMB No. 0938-0787

REQUEST FOR EMPLOYMENT INFORMATION

SECTION A: To be completed by individual signing up for Medicare Part B (Medical Insurance)

1. Employer's Name
2. Date ☐☐/☐☐/☐☐☐☐
3. Employer's Address

City State ☐☐ Zip Code ☐☐☐☐☐

4. Applicant's Name
5. Applicant's Social Security Number ☐☐☐-☐☐-☐☐☐☐
6. Employee's Name
7. Employee's Social Security Number ☐☐☐-☐☐-☐☐☐☐

SECTION B: To be completed by Employers

For Employer Group Health Plans ONLY:

1. Is (or was) the applicant covered under an employer group health plan? ☐ Yes ☐ No
2. If yes, give the date the applicant's coverage began. (mm/yyyy) ☐☐/☐☐☐☐
3. Has the coverage ended? ☐ Yes ☐ No
4. If yes, give the date the coverage ended. (mm/yyyy) ☐☐/☐☐☐☐
5. When did the employee work for your company?
From: (mm/yyyy) ☐☐/☐☐☐☐ To: (mm/yyyy) ☐☐/☐☐☐☐ Still Employed: (mm/yyyy) ☐☐/☐☐☐☐
6. If you're a large group health plan and the applicant is disabled, please list the timeframe (all months) that your group health plan was primary payer.
From: (mm/yyyy) ☐☐/☐☐☐☐ To: (mm/yyyy) ☐☐/☐☐☐☐

For Hours Bank Arrangements ONLY:

1. Is (or was) the applicant covered under an Hours Bank Arrangement? ☐ Yes ☐ No
2. If yes, does the applicant have hours remaining in reserve? ☐ Yes ☐ No
3. Date reserve hours ended or will be used? (mm/yyyy) ☐☐/☐☐☐☐

2. **Form #2 Application for Enrollment in Medicare:** this is your application for medical insurance from Medicare known as Part B. Social Security fills out this form

Below is a Sample of what the form looks like.

DEPARTMENT OF HEALTH AND HUMAN SERVICES
CENTERS FOR MEDICARE & MEDICAID SERVICES

Form Approved
OMB No. 0938-1230

APPLICATION FOR ENROLLMENT IN MEDICARE PART B (MEDICAL INSURANCE)

1. Your Social Security Claim Number ☐☐☐-☐☐-☐☐☐☐ Beneficiary Identification Code (BIC) ☐☐☐
2. Do you wish to sign up for Medicare Part B (Medical Insurance)? ☐ YES
3. Your Name (Last Name, First Name, Middle Name)
4. Mailing Address (Number and Street, P.O. Box, or Route)
5. City State ☐☐ Zip Code ☐☐☐☐☐
6. Phone Number (including area code) (☐☐☐) ☐☐☐-☐☐☐☐
7. Written Signature (DO NOT PRINT)
SIGN HERE
8. Date Signed ☐☐/☐☐/☐☐☐☐

IF THIS APPLICATION HAS BEEN SIGNED BY MARK (X), A WITNESS WHO KNOWS THE APPLICANT MUST SUPPLY THE INFORMATION REQUESTED BELOW.

9. Signature of Witness
10. Date Signed ☐☐/☐☐/☐☐☐☐
11. Address of Witness
12. Remarks

Once the employment form is signed by your company, take both forms to your local Social Security office for your Medicare to begin when you have retired. You can mail your forms back to Social Security, but the wait is longer to receive your Medicare card with both Parts A and B

Rules for Enrolling in COBRA Past 65

Medicare Part B Nightmare Began with Enrolling in COBRA!
Toni

My Medicare and Social Security nightmare began when I retired from my job, July 31 of last year and enrolled in COBRA so that I could have a knee replacement in December. I was given inaccurate information from a local Social Security agent and now I am going to receive a penalty because I did not enroll in Part B at the right time

I am 69 and have been employed by 3 different companies since I turned 65. No one ever informed me that I needed to have a special form signed by each company I worked for since turning 65

I spoke to the assistant district manager of the Social Security office and she asked me why I never enrolled in Medicare's Parts A & B when I left the company and enrolled in COBRA. I was informed that my penalty is 40%, which is 69-65 or 4 years. The penalty is not for 1 year, but forever!!

I now have to fight for "reconsideration" from Social Security because they are under the impression that I have waited past the 8-month window to enroll in Medicare

Please inform your readers how important it is to enroll in Part B when enrolling in COBRA

Cathie from Ventura, Ca

Hello Cathie

The majority of Americans do not realize how important it is to enroll the right way and now that many are leaving or losing their jobs after 65, they are finding a gigantic surprise when they enroll in Medicare Part B after being on COBRA.

At the Toni Says® office, we inform those who come to the office for Medicare planning to be sure that ***Part B begins the day you lose your company benefits or the day your COBRA plan starts.***

In the Medicare and You Handbook under "Should I get Part B?" it discusses the rules of COBRA when you were first eligible and what the late penalties are. Many think the Part B rule starts when COBRA ends in 18 months

They are not aware that the ***Special Enrollment Period*** begins the month they lose their company benefits or employment ends and they go on COBRA. They try to enroll in Part B like you did Cathie, with a BIG SURPRISE, finding they are penalized 10% each year or 12-month period, you could have had Part B, but didn't. The penalty goes all the way back to the day he/she turned 65 or the day Part A began.

I have a client in Wharton, TX, 79 years old and was always on his wife's company health plan. He never enrolled in Part B because she was the "working spouse" but she lost her job. She was 62 and because she had health issues and the cost of COBRA was less than an Obamacare health plan, she enrolled herself and her 79-year-old husband in COBRA. When COBRA ended 18 months later, they went to Social Security to enroll him in Part B and were shocked!!! His premium for Part B premium for that year was $104.90 (The monthly premiums are subject to change each year). Take 79-65 which is 14 years and so this elderly gentleman now has a 14-year penalty or 140% forever. His Part B premium for that year was $104.90 plus $146.86 penalty for late enrollment for a total of $251.76 per month. This is a 140% penalty (14 years x 10%) each month for the rest of his Medicare life. He did not enroll in "Part B" at the right time!

Toni Says® always have Part B in place when leaving your job or losing your company benefits and not being enrolled in "true employer benefits". There might not be a second chance

Medicare and Social Security do not recognize COBRA as health coverage based on current employment.

Do I Need Part B When Choosing COBRA?

When should someone enroll in Part B when enrolling on COBRA? Can you wait until you are no longer on COBRA to enroll in Part B?

The answer is simple. You should not wait to enroll in Part B. Make sure that your Part B begins the day you lose your company benefits or the day your COBRA plan starts

There is a time limit to enroll in Part B and not be subject to the 10% penalty per 12-month period. The Medicare and You Handbook tells us "How to Enroll in Parts A and/or Part B when you were first eligible and what the late penalties are.

Many think the Part B rule starts when COBRA ends in 18 months. They are not aware that the ***Special Enrollment Period*"** begins the month after they lose their company benefits or employment ends and they go on COBRA.

Many enroll in Part B with a BIG SURPRISE, finding they are penalized 10% each year or 12-month period, they could have had Part B, but didn't. The penalty goes all the way back to the day he/she turned 65 or the day Part A began and doesn't go away for the balance of their Medicare life. If you are 68, when you go to Social Security and sign up for Medicare for the first time, subtract 68-65 which is 3 years times 10%. There will be a 30% additional penalty on your Part B premium forever. All of the arguing with Social Security won't help, it's the rule and that is their job to enforce the rules...and they do it!!

The Medicare and You Handbook explains the ***Special Enrollment Period*** (SEP) for those who did not sign up for Part A and/or Part B when first eligible as "during the 8-month period that begins the month after the employment ends or the group health plan coverage ends, whichever happens first". After this 8-month period, the 10% penalty can begin. It does not say when COBRA ends

My advice is to always have Part B in place when leaving your job or losing your company benefits. Part B is so important because it covers so much of your health care and if you do not have Part B, then you will pay 100% out of your own pocket for what it covers.

I Retired COBRA Was NOT the BEST Choice for My Husband's Medicare!!

Dear Toni

I am a 62-year-old, who was a Vice President of the company which I retired. My husband is 75 and I have always carried him on my company health insurance policy. I was advised to enroll John in COBRA when I retired, and now our Medicare nightmare has escalated to my husband not being able to enroll in Medicare when COBRA ends this September

Now I am finding out that there will be a penalty for John not enrolling in Part B when he should have and he will not have Part B until he enrolls after January 1, and his Part B will not begin until July

1. What is he to do for doctor, outpatient surgery or anything under Medicare Part B since he will have none of the benefits from September to July 1st. No one has ever told us when the time limit is and I have never received a Medicare and You Handbook, because I am 62 not 65. We didn't know the rules were in the handbook until I began reading your column

Please let your readers know how important it is to enroll in Medicare Part B at the correct time...

Carla from Miami, FL

Good Morning Carla:

You are right, people should not wait to enroll in Part B when retiring and enrolling in COBRA! Not only is not having Part B to lean on costly, but the penalties for Part B are very costly.

Social Security keeps track of your records, when you are past 65, and you have delayed your Part B. When you decided to retire, you must get your company's HR department to sign off on the Social Security form "Request for Employment Information", for your husband to show he was covered by your company's health insurance (which is "creditable" coverage). If that form is not filled out properly and taken to the Social Security office (to apply for Medicare) within the correct amount of time **(63 days)** the potential Medicare Beneficiary can receive a 10% penalty for every 12-month period that they could have been on Medicare Part B, but failed to enroll.

Always, make sure that your Medicare Part B begins the day you lose your company benefits or the day your COBRA plan starts. The Medicare and You Handbook, under "Should I get Part B?", lets you know when you were first eligible and what the late penalties a

Many think the Part B rule starts when COBRA ends in 18 months. They are not aware that the ***Special Enrollment Period*** " begins the month they lose their company benefits or employment ends and go on COBRA.

Many enroll in Part B with a STICKER SHOCK, like you have in regard to your husband's Medicare and are penalized. Arguing with Social Security won't help, "THEM'S THE RULES."

Toni Says® **Always** have Part B in place when leaving your job or losing your company benefits. Do not wait

You will be charged the Medicare Part B penalty each month, as long as you are on Medicare or have passed away. The penalty will last the rest of your lifetime. You must get this right the first time! There might not be a second chance!

Why Did Enrolling in COBRA Cost Me $40K I Did Not Have a Chance to Enroll in Medicare Part B?

Reader Alert Many company benefit plans terminate the day you are no longer working full-time. Explore you or your spouse's group medical plan rules and options with Medicare if you are 65 or older.

Morning Toni:

My wife and I desperately need your guidance because this March, I was rushed to the ER because of kidney failure, which was caused from stage 4 of prostate cancer that has now spread to my pelvic bones

Because I was working full-time, I took a leave of absence and short-term disability in March for 60 days while receiving my cancer treatment. Short term disability ended on June 24th and so I was placed on long term disability

I was informed via a phone call to my hospital room at MD Anderson that I had qualified for long term disability, would no longer be part of the company's health plan and that COBRA would begin immediately

My wife and I enrolled and paid for COBRA, so that I could continue with medical care from MD Anderson. It took 6 weeks to get the paperwork to Social Security for me to enroll in Part B, since I was not working full-time and my Medicare Part B began August 1st

Now my Cobra nightmare begins because COBRA is only paying the 20% of medical/ doctor bills and I was billed the 80% because I was not enrolled in Medicare Part B which has totaled over $40K. Please help me with what I need to do…

Thanks, Robert NW Houston area

Robert

The Toni Says® team will do all that we can to help you solve this problem of your` $40K Medicare Part B medical bills

Those reading this article need to realize the seriousness of Medicare and insurance rules

The Medicare and You Handbook discusses the topics of "***Special Enrollment Period***" and "Should I Get Part B". It states, "You have 8 months to sign up without a penalty. **This period will run whether or not you choose COBRA. If you choose COBRA, don't wait until your COBRA ends to enroll in Part B**"

Robert, you did everything correctly by going to Social Security and taking them the "Request for Employment Information" form signed by your HR. You were within the correct time limits

You are in an insurance "glitch" and they are using "Coordination of Benefits" as their ruling.

Group health insurance plans are a state specific regulated industry not a Medicare regulated plan. Since you are past 65, the health plan is passing the 80% of the doctor/medical bills to Medicare

I am seeing a change in group health plans with many not covering employees past their last day of work. Unfortunately, you are in the middle of a healthcare crisis, when technically you went from full-time employee to a part-time employee because I know you and your company want you to return back to work as a full-time employee.

I am a Medicare advocate and consultant, but if there are HCN/Houston Chronicle readers of this column who are attorneys or have experienced with this type of issue, please email me personally at toni@tonisays.com and I will give your information to Robert who needs all of our help and prayers to get through this trying personal time when he should be playing with his grandkids.

Working with Company Benefits and Totally Overwhelmed!

Hello Toni:

Your name was given to me by my company's benefits administrator in North Carolina to assist me with my Medicare options. I turned 65 last December, and now I am concerned because our group company benefits are Blue Cross/Blue Shield of North Carolina and I work and live in the Houston

My concern is that I am an adult diabetic and I could lose my doctors because of healthcare reform and that I should get on Medicare ASAP

I currently take 10 prescriptions for cardiovascular issues and an insulin diabetic with expensive diabetic meds. I'm concerned I may be receiving a penalty because I never did sign up for Medicare. Should I have signed up for Medicare Part B because I began my Part A when I turned 65?

Garth from Southwest Houston, TX

Garth

Don't worry! The **good news** is you have protection regarding receiving a Medicare Part B and even D penalty because you have "true" company benefits.

Until you retire, you do not have to do a thing regarding your Medicare unless you lose your company health benefits

The most important item to discuss when someone is either turning 65 or retiring past 65, is what prescriptions you are currently taking. With you being an insulin dependent diabetic, at the Toni Says® office, we perform customized Medicare health and prescription drug consultation.

My concern is with 10 prescriptions, when you decide to retire or your company decides to retire you, if you go on Medicare with a Medicare Supplement and Part D prescription drug plan, you could go in the prescription drug donut hole quick. As it is currently, because you are still covered by your "true" company benefits you have the protection of no "donut hole". Your company health plan meets Medicare's creditable prescription drug coverage that pays on average at least as much as Medicare's standard prescription drug plan does.

You are **"still working"** and those are magic words when it comes to enrolling past 65 and losing your company benefits. The Medicare and You Handbook, discusses leaving your group benefits and "that you can sign up for Part B anytime during the 8-month period that begins the month after the employment ends or the coverage ends, whichever happens first".

When we perform a Medicare planning consultation at the Toni Says® office, whether just laid off or retiring, we stress the value of getting Part B for the first time

The process to enroll in Medicare Part B, if you have delayed it is

- There are 2 forms available from Social Security's website or you can ask from the Toni Says® office. (toni@tonisays.com) On the top of each form write in ***red letters "Special Enrollment Period".*** This tells the Social Security agent that is processing them, you are signing up at the right time and keeps from giving you a penalty. You are applying for a **SEP (*Special Enrollment Period*).**

. **Form #1 Request for Employment Information:** proof of group health care coverage based on current employment. If you have had 2 or more jobs since turning 65, then all companies you have worked for from age 65 to the time you are retiring, to sign this form. If you are married, you will need the same number of forms filled out and signed by the companies HR departments for which you have worked, proving your spouse was covered by company insurance (if they are on Medicare or Medicare eligible)

Below is a Sample of what the form looks like.

Special Enrollment Period

DEPARTMENT OF HEALTH AND HUMAN SERVICES
CENTERS FOR MEDICARE & MEDICAID SERVICES

Form Approved
OMB No. 0938-0787

REQUEST FOR EMPLOYMENT INFORMATION

SECTION A: To be completed by individual signing up for Medicare Part B (Medical Insurance)

1. Employer's Name
2. Date ☐☐/☐☐/☐☐☐☐
3. Employer's Address

City — State ☐☐ — Zip Code ☐☐☐☐☐

4. Applicant's Name
5. Applicant's Social Security Number ☐☐☐-☐☐-☐☐☐☐
6. Employee's Name
7. Employee's Social Security Number ☐☐☐-☐☐-☐☐☐☐

SECTION B: To be completed by Employers

For Employer Group Health Plans ONLY:

1. Is (or was) the applicant covered under an employer group health plan? ☐ Yes ☐ No
2. If yes, give the date the applicant's coverage began. (mm/yyyy) ☐☐/☐☐☐☐
3. Has the coverage ended? ☐ Yes ☐ No
4. If yes, give the date the coverage ended. (mm/yyyy) ☐☐/☐☐☐☐
5. When did the employee work for your company?
From: (mm/yyyy) ☐☐/☐☐☐☐ To: (mm/yyyy) ☐☐/☐☐☐☐ Still Employed: (mm/yyyy) ☐☐/☐☐☐☐
6. If you're a large group health plan and the applicant is disabled, please list the timeframe (all months) that your group health plan was primary payer.
From: (mm/yyyy) ☐☐/☐☐☐☐ To: (mm/yyyy) ☐☐/☐☐☐☐

2. **Form #2 Application for Enrollment in Medicare:** this is your application for medical insurance from Medicare known as Part B. Social Security fills out this form

Below is a Sample of what the form looks like.

DEPARTMENT OF HEALTH AND HUMAN SERVICES
CENTERS FOR MEDICARE & MEDICAID SERVICES

Form Approved
OMB No. 0938-1230

APPLICATION FOR ENROLLMENT IN MEDICARE PART B (MEDICAL INSURANCE)

1. Your Social Security Claim Number ☐☐☐-☐☐-☐☐☐☐ — Beneficiary Identification Code (BIC) ☐☐☐
2. Do you wish to sign up for Medicare Part B (Medical Insurance)? ☐ YES
3. Your Name (Last Name, First Name, Middle Name)
4. Mailing Address (Number and Street, P.O. Box, or Route)
5. City — State ☐☐ — Zip Code ☐☐☐☐☐
6. Phone Number (including area code) (☐☐☐) ☐☐☐-☐☐☐☐
7. Written Signature (DO NOT PRINT)
SIGN HERE
8. Date Signed ☐☐/☐☐/☐☐☐☐

IF THIS APPLICATION HAS BEEN SIGNED BY MARK (X), A WITNESS WHO KNOWS THE APPLICANT MUST SUPPLY THE INFORMATION REQUESTED BELOW.

9. Signature of Witness
10. Date Signed ☐☐/☐☐/☐☐☐☐
11. Address of Witness
12. Remarks

Once the form(s) are signed by your company HR, take both forms to your local Social Security office for your Medicare to begin when you have retired.

When leaving company benefits, there is an **8-month** window for Medicare Part B enrollment and **63 days** to receive Medicare Prescription Drug Part D plan without receiving a penalty.

Medicare's…Enrollment Check-List!

Hello Toni:

My husband, David, has been laid off because of what is happening to oil companies in the Houston area. He is 68 and has never enrolled in Medicare, but I am turning 65 in November. We both are covered under his employer's health plan and it is ending on October 31st

We have been told that he will get a penalty because he is over 65 and never enrolled in Part B. I assume that I am ok since I turn 65 in November. Please explain what our options are since we are different ages

Thanks, Peggy from Bellaire, TX

Great Question, Peggy:

There are 2 different rules regarding enrolling in Medicare Parts A and B in your household.

David needs to apply for a SEP (**Special Enrollment Period**) by downloading the form OMB #0938 (request for employer's information) from **socialsecurity.gov** or email info@tonisays.com and we can email you a form.

Have David's HR department sign off on the form in October and take the form in person to your local Social Security department to apply for Medicare Parts A and B. Advise the Social Security representative that he is losing his company benefits and need his Medicare Parts A and B to begin November 1 t

For you, Peggy, enrolling in Medicare is simple and very different from David's because you are turning 65 in November. You need to go online at www.socialsecurity.gov/benefits/medicare only 90 days prior to turning 65 and apply online for a November 1 t effective date

Below is a check-list for those enrolling in Medicare the correct way:

1) Learn that Original Medicare: Part A covers your in-patient hospital stay, skilled nursing/rehab stay, blood transfusions, home health and hospice. Original Medicare: Part B covers your primary care or specialist whether in the office or performing surgery, outpatient surgery, durable medical equipment, x-rays, CAT scans, MRIs, chemotherapy, etc. Discuss with your doctor about what they accept such as Original/Traditional Medicare or a Medicare Part C (Medicare Advantage plan).
2) Explore your Medicare Advantage plan options such as HMO, PPO or PFFS
3) Go to the specific Medicare Advantage plan's hospital/provider online directory to be sure your physicians and hospitals are available for you. Remember online directories are more accurate than printed copies, since many providers may have already opted out of accepting that specific plan.
4) Shop for a Medicare Supplement/Medigap policy. Start seeking a Medicare Supplement by talking with your doctor

5) Seek Medicare Prescription Drug planning every year to see if your standalone Prescription Drug or Medicare Advantage Plan with prescriptions formulary covers all of your brand name orgeneric prescription drugs.
6) Seek "Extra Help" with prescription drugs if you meet low-income qualifications.
7) Consider a Long-Term Care (LTC) option such as standalone LTC policies, hybrid annuities or life insurance with LTC riders, VA aid and attendant benefits or applying for financial help from your specific states Medicaid for LTC.
8) Make sure your legal documents are in order such as power of attorney, medical power of attorney and living will.

Notes

Chapter 2
Original/Traditional Medicare
Medicare Parts A & B
Medicare Part A Costs for 2022

(Costs change every January 1)

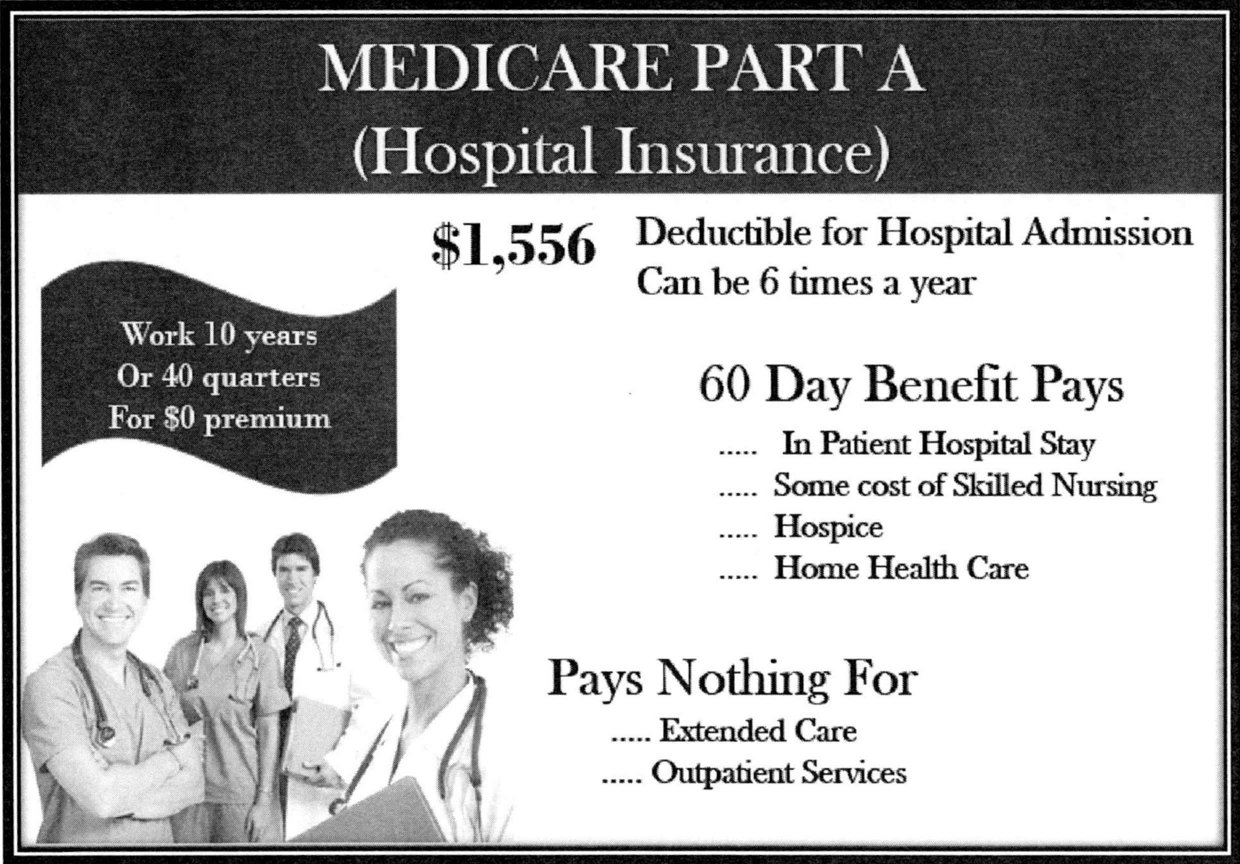

<u>MEDICARE PART A</u> (Hospital Insurance)

Part A pays for your care while you are in the hospital. The in-patient hospital co-pay changes every year and is a 60-day benefit. The in-patient hospital co-pay can be 6 times a year. Part A also pays some of the costs if you stay in a skilled nursing facility or are receiving blood transfusions. Hospice and home health care are provided under Medicare Part A and co-pays and deductibles may apply. More specifics on Part A and how it can affect your pocketbook are explained later in this chapter.

MEDICARE PART A

Expenses Incurred for	Medicare Covers:	You Pay:
Hospital Stays	Most confinement costs After the required Medicare deductible	**DEDUCTIBLE** (Changes/Increases each year.) **This could happen several times a year.**
Blood	Cost of blood from Pint # 4	You must pay **100%** for the first 3 pints of blood.
Home Health Care	100% as long as you use a Medicare certified Home Health Agency.	**$0** for home health services **20%** of the Medicare-Approved Amount for durable medical equipment if you are at home
Hospice Care	For people with a terminal illness who are expected to live 6 months or less. Coverage includes drugs, medical and support services from a Medicare approved hospice, plus additional services including grief counseling for the patient and their family.	Co-pays and deductibles may apply.
Skilled Nursing Facility Review the 2017 New Medicare Outpatient Observation Notice (MOON) article page 36 of this chapter	Medicare pays **100%** for the first **20 days** that you **REQUIRE Skilled Nursing Care.** **21 – 100** days patient pays a **per day co-payment**	**$0** for the first **20 days** that you **REQUIRE skilled nursing care.** **21 – 100** days patient pays a **per day co-payment** *Be sure to receive your "**MOON**" form during an inpatient hospital stay. Verify if this is an inpatient or outpatient stay for Medicare to pay for the skilled nursing charges. Very important!

What is Part A? *(Hospital Insurance)*

Part A is the in-hospital part of Original Medicare. Most people do not have to pay for Part A. You or your spouse must have worked at least 10 years (*40 quarters*) paying into the social security system to receive Part A premium free.

Toni Says® *Usually, Part A begins the first day of the month you turn 65 and are enrolled in Medicare or the 25th month if you are under 65 and receiving Social Security benefits. For those not receiving Social Security benefits prior to turning 65, you must go to Social Security 3 months prior to turning 65 and enroll in Medicare. To be sure your Part A begins the month you turn 65. This is Very Important!!*

What does Part A Pay for?

Blood – Starting with the 4th pint of Blood *(you got it...pints 1-3 are on you and who knows what it costs!)*

Home Health Care - Has to be ordered by a doctor and must be a certified Medicare Home Health Agency. There is no deductible or co-pay for home health care when using the right agency and it must meet a set of very specific criteria in order for Medicare to cover it

Hospice Care – Is for those with a terminal illness that are expected to live 6 months or less if the disease runs its normal course. You must use a Medicare-Approved Hospice agency. Coverage includes drugs, medical, and supports (grief counseling for terminal and related conditions). This care is usually done in the home

Hospital Stay - The in-hospital stay is where you put your head on a pillow and spend the night. The stay is a 60-day benefit only. This means that the deductible can be used 6 times a year. You are charged a deductible each time you go in the hospital unless you go more than 1 time in a 60-day period.

All costs while in the hospital such as semi-private room, meals, general nursing, and other hospital services and supplies are included. Private room *(unless medically necessary)* private duty nursing, telephone and television are not medically necessary, and you must pay the difference for them. Deductibles change every year so check the chart at the end of you Medicare and You Handbook or visit my web site www.tonisays.com for any current changes to Medicare.

Skilled Nursing Facility - To qualify for a skilled nursing facility, you must have a 3-day hospital stay not 1 or 2 but 3 complete days and Medicare does count them. Once admitted to a skilled nursing facility, you must require the skills of a nurse *(IVs feeding tube, etc.)* or require physical or speech therapy. You could possibly have up to 100 days, provided you need skilled nursing or you demonstrate significant medical improvement. Medicare pays your first 20 days in full. Days 21-100 have a co-pay each day and that amount changes each year. This co-pay will come out of your pocket!! At the end of your skilled nursing stay you can be discharged home, or you can move to a private pay bed in the facility. Either way you must pay 100% totally out of YOUR pocket unless you have purchased a Long-Term Care policy that can help to pick up the costs. Even though this benefit is up to 100 days, it does not mean you get 100 days automatically. If you only need personal care (*such as bathing, eating, or dressing*) or custodial care (*such as someone to watch over you*) you no longer meet the Medicare requirement for skilled care. A Long-Term Care policy would help to pay for those costs.

Medicare Part B Costs for 2022

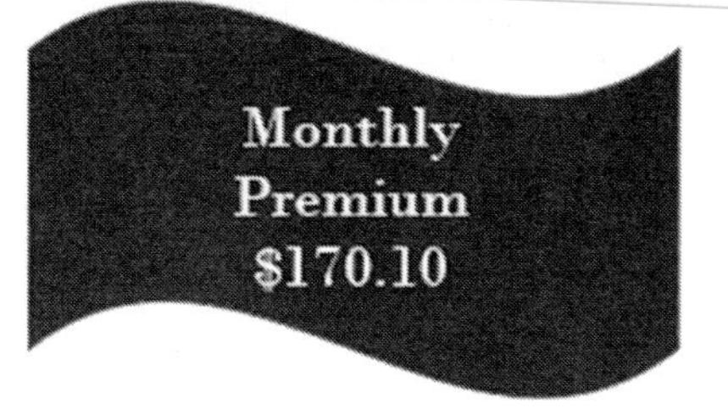

$233 Deductible (Per Calendar Year)
One Deductible

Medicare pays: 80%
You pay: 20%

... Medically necessary services
... Doctors, MRIs, Heart Scans
... Medical Equipment
... Outpatient care and Preventative services

MEDICARE PART B (Medical Insurance)

Part B pays for medically necessary services such as doctors' services, outpatient hospital care, and home health care that Part A does not pay for. It also helps pay for some preventive services *("some" but not all preventive services)* More on what Part B covers in this chapter.

MEDICARE PART B

Expenses Incurred for:	Medicare Covers:	You Pay Deductible PLUS:
Medical Expenses **physician's services** for **In-patient and outpatient** medical/surgical services; Physical or Speech therapy, diagnostic tests.	Generally, **80%** of approved amount (Subject to Part B deductible)	**20%** of Medicare approved amount YOU pay for. **There is no limit** for the **20%**
Clinical Laboratory Services Blood tests, urinalysis	Generally, **100%** of Medicare Approved Amount (Subject to Part B deductible)	Nothing for Services
Home Health Care Part-time or intermittent skilled care, home health aide services, Durable medical supplies and other services	Generally **100%** of the Medicare Approved Amount (Subject to Part B deductible)	Generally, **$0** for home healthservices **20%** of the Medicare-Approved Amount for durable medical equipment if you are at home
Outpatient Hospital Treatment Hospital services for the diagnosis or treatment of an illness or injury	Generally, **80%** of Medicare Approved Amount (Subject to Part B deductible)	Generally, **20%** of the Medicare Approved amount YOU pay. **There is No limit** for the **20%.** Or fixed co-pay not to exceed the Part A hospital deductible
Blood	After the first 3 pints of blood, **80%** of the Medicare approved amount (Subject to Part B deductible)	First 3 pints of blood YOU pay plus **20%** of approved amount for additional pints.

What is Part B? (*Medicare Insurance*)

Part B is the Medical part of Medicare and pays doctor visits, surgery bills, X-rays, Labs, MRIs, outpatient hospital visits, emergency room visits, or anything that is not in-patient hospital care. Part B also covers Preventative Services. (*See lists of Preventative Services at the end of this guide*). Unlike Part A, Part B's premium is deducted each month from your social security check. This amount changes every year. If you decide NOT TO TAKE Medicare Part B because you can't afford the monthly premium or you don't get sick, because you've always been healthy as a horse Think again!! You will pay 100%of your doctor/out-patient hospital services out of your own pocket, by not enrolling in Part B; you havejust given away everything that Part B provides! There are no exceptions to this rule, so make sure when you get ready to get on Medicare that you take Part B. VERY IMPORTANT!!! Uncle Sam has theattitude "You can pay me now or pay more later." Not enrolling at the right time, you will be penalized10% penalty each year that you could have had Part B, for the rest of your Medicare life. 1 year = 10%3 years = 30% 5 years = 50%

Toni Says® *Usually, Part B begins the first day of the month you turn 65 and are enrolled in Medicare or the 25th month if you are under 65 and receiving Social Security benefits. For those not receiving Social Security benefits prior to turning 65, you must go to Social Security 3 months prior to turning 65 and enroll in Medicare or online at* **www.socialsecurity.gov/benefits/medicare**. *To be sure your Part B begins the month you turn 65. This is Very Important!!*

What does Part B pay for?

Medical and Other Services – Medicare pays generally 80% and you pay generally 20% of the Medicare Approved amount for most physician services for inpatient and outpatient hospital care. There is no limit to how much the 20% can be. *(Example surgeon, doctor visits, anesthesiologist, pathologists, second surgical opinion etc.)*

Clinical Laboratory Services - blood tests, urinalysis, x-rays no co-pay.

Home Health Care - home health care is part-time or intermediate skilled care, or home health aide services that must be from a Medicare Approved home health agency. There is no co pay.

Durable Medical Equipment and Other Services – Medicare pays generally 80% and you pay generally 20% for supplies like wheel chairs, hospital beds, walkers, oxygen etc. Other services include prosthetic devices such as artificial arms, legs, etc.

Blood - After the first 3 pints of blood, Medicare pays 80% and you pay generally 20% of the approved amount for additional pints of blood. Who knows what the cost of blood is? The cost of blood is different at individual hospitals.

***Note** - One more important thing for you to remember is that doctors or suppliers must agree to accept Medicare Assignment. This means, that the patient will not be required to pay any expense, in excess of Medicare's approved charge.

Reader Alert Doctors who do not accept Medicare Assignment can charge 115% more than the Medicare Approved amount. Some doctors may not even take Medicare and you will pay the entire amount out of your pocket and be reimbursed from Medicare, but who knows how long getting reimbursed will take

Toni Says® *Make sure that you check to see if your doctor takes Medicare. Not all doctors do and they will make you pay at the window when leaving!!!!*

Search through the table of contents for your specific Original Medicare (Medicare Parts A and/ or Part B questions) or read the rest of this chapter and gain Original Medicare knowledge to help your friends that are confused. Below are articles from the Toni Says® newspaper column regarding specific questions about Original Medicare.

Original or Traditional Medicare...What is the Difference?

Good Morning Ms. Toni:

I am turning 65 in Dec. and retiring because of my health. I recently had a triple bi-pass and last week I talked with the office manager at my cardiologist's office about me getting on Medicare and what I should do?

She said for me to enroll in "Traditional Medicare." I have no idea what "Traditional Medicare" is. I cannot find Traditional Medicare anywhere in the Medicare and You Handbook*? Is that a certain insurance plan?*

I do not want to enroll in the wrong plan and totally mess up my Medicare

Thank You, Samuel, a confused reader

Hello Samuel

I will make this as simple as I can. I have consulted with confused Americans who have a PHD in higher education and understanding Medicare frustrates them too

Let's examine just what "Original or Traditional Medicare" is?

Most healthcare professionals and their office staff call Medicare, "Traditional" Medicare, but Medicare refers to the government health plan for those 65 or older, under 65 with certain disabilities or those with end stage renal disease (kidney dialysis) as "Original" Medicare. You will not find "Traditional" Medicare anywhere on the medicare.gov website or in the Medicare and You Handbook, but the two are the same

"Original" or "Traditional" Medicare consists of Parts A and B only! **NOT** the rest of the alphabet soup, Parts C or D.

Original/Traditional Medicare is also known as your Medicare card or as many refers to the card as the *red, white and blue card"*. There is not a network with Original/Traditional Medicare. If your doctor or healthcare provider accepts Original Medicare or Medicare assignment, then they will accept Traditional Medicare because they are the same thing.

Original/Traditional Medicare Parts A and B are explained below

MEDICARE PART A (In-patient Hospital Insurance) pays for your medical care with an in-patient hospital stay. Part A also pays some of the costs if you stay in a skilled nursing facility which has 100-day benefit, hospice, or if you receive home health care. The Part A deductible changes every year and can be used **6 times 6 deductibles** in a year. Yes, Part A has a benefit period of 60 days, so every 60 days; there is a new deductible.

Skilled nursing has a $0 co-pay for days 1-20, but from days 21-100, there is specific co pay per day which also changes every year. After day 100, you pay all the cost for each additional day. And **YES**, the skilled nursing facility will invoice you the additional cost.

MEDICARE PART B (Medical Insurance) helps cover for medically necessary services such as doctors' services, office visits including doctor charges for surgery for an in-patient hospital stay, all outpatient hospital care/services, tests, durable medical equipment (wheelchairs walkers, oxygen, and other medical services. Part B has a monthly premium which also changes every year.

✍***Note** Part B and Part D premiums are now based on income, not everyone pays the same amount!!

Part B has a yearly deductible that also changes every year. Once the calendar year deductible has been met; Medicare pays 80% of the Medicare approved amount and you or whoever is on Medicare, will pay 20% of the Medicare approved amount.

Original/Traditional Medicare have some gaps and you can fill the gaps with a Medicare Supplement/ Medigap Plan that works directly with Original/Traditional Medicare, but the Medicare Supplement/ Medigap has a premium.

New Inpatient/Outpatient Rule for Medicare

Toni Says Newsletter Alert: Around October 1, the 2018 Medicare & You handbook should have arrived in everyone's mailbox with a surprise on page 32 titled, "Am I an inpatient or outpatient?" if you are currently on Medicare.

What does that mean? Let's discuss it...

A new Medicare rule called **Medicare Outpatient Observation Notice (MOON)** went into effect on Wednesday, March 8th, and applies to those with an Original Medicare hospital stay. It does not apply to those with Medicare Advantage plans.

This new rule is explained differently and with more details than when first released last March, and in the 2018 Medicare and You handbook, it states in the entire passage....

> *"Staying overnight in a hospital doesn't always mean you're an inpatient. You only become an inpatient when a **hospital formally** admits you as an **inpatient**, after a **doctor orders it**. You're still an **outpatient** if you haven't been **formally admitted inpatient**, even if you're getting emergency department services, observation services, outpatient surgery, lab tests, or X-rays. **You or a family member should always ask if you're an inpatient oran outpatient each day during your stay, since it affects what you pay and can affect whether you'll qualify for Part A coverage in a skilled nursing facility.**"*

Last March when the Toni Says® office became aware of the new MOON (Medicare Outpatient Observation Notice), the law read that "beginning March 8th, hospitals and critical access hospitals must provide the **MOON** (Medicare Outpatient Observation Notice) to Medicare beneficiaries or their legal representative if receiving observation services as an outpatient for more than 24 hours. The **MOON** must be provided in written form that is signed and dated with an oral explanation from the facility no later than 36 hours from the time the Medicare patient begins receiving outpatient observation services. This time limit is considered the new two midnight stay observation policy."

It seems that on page 32 of the Medicare & You handbook that one who is having a hospital stay should be more involved or one may have to pay more if they happen to need a skilled nursing stay.

When I read page 32, I knew that many on Medicare would not see this information and may have to pay thousands of dollars for additional hospital or skilled nursing care.

Below is what you should know when having a hospital stay and what you may want to inform your family members or caregivers:

. Remember the **MOON** rule applies to those on **"Original Medicare"** and not Medicare Advantage plans, as Medicare Advantage Plans have their own rules and options regarding inpatient/outpatient services
2. Discuss your hospital procedure with your physician/surgeon regarding whether this will be an inpatient or outpatient stay.
3. Remember you only become an inpatient once the hospital, not your doctor, "formally admits" you with a doctor's order.
4. You or a family member should **ask every day** if you or your loved one is an **inpatient outpatient**. (This information was highlighted on page 32 meaning it is important!)
5. Read on page 32 regarding the Medicare Outpatient Observation Notice (MOON), which advises you if you are in an outpatient rather than inpatient status while in the hospital.
6. Know that outpatient status does not cover any skilled nursing costs.

Part A-In-Patient Hospital Coverage articles

Bad Medicare Part A Information Cost Me $5000 a Year!

Hi Toni

I am 65 almost 66, "still working" and covered entirely by my company with a HSA insurance plan. I put about $5,000 per year into a tax-sheltered account for medical expenses

When I went to the SS office to discuss my Medicare and they convinced me to sign up for Medicare Part A

Now I find out that since my insurance is a HSA, signing up for Part A may disqualify me for the tax-free savings plan

1. *Does having Part A really disqualify me from contributing the $5000 to my HSA Plan?*
2. *Should I go to the SS office and stop Medicare part A?*
3. *Can I get back into Part A when I retire?*

Thanks, Carl, Lake Charles, LA

Hello Carl

Social Security says that Medicare Part A (hospital) begins when Social Security knows you have turned 65 not Medicare. I would advise you or anyone who wants to delay their Medicare that they **must** be working full time as an employee, not self-employed or a contracted worker and be covered under a group health plan based on current employment not an individual health plan.

Below are the answers to your questions about enrolling in Medicare when you have a HSA:

. **Medicare Part A and HSA** Yes, enrolling in Medicare Part A can disqualify you from contributing the $5000 to your HSA. It does not matter if you are contributing or your employer is contributing. Always talk with your HR department, contact your insurance company when you are contemplating what to do with your Medicare coverage if it is different from the norm or you can always contact me at **info@tonisays.com** and together we can explore all of your options.

2. **Stopping your Medicare Part A:** I would call Social Security at 1/800-772-1213 and explain to the agent how you were misinformed since you have been enrolled and funded your HSA before you turned 65 and now you cannot contribute to the plan. Ask if you can appeal what was advised to you and you need to schedule an appointment with your local office.
3. **Getting Part A back:** When you call Social Security to schedule an appointment ask them what type of problems you would have in getting back into Part A at a later date. This is the first I have heard of someone wanting to stop their Part A. I've seen many who have stopped Medicare Part B (Medical) when they have returned to work with group health insurance.

For those who need to delay Medicare Part A, due to "still working fulltime" with company health insurance which includes an HSA and want to continue making contributions to the HSA, can do so by simply not informing Social Security that you have turned 65. When you do contact Social Security to begin receiving your Social Security check or to enroll in Medicare Part A and/or Part B, it is then that you cannot make any more contributions to the HSA because you will be in Medicare.

Your Medicare Part A and/or Part B dates will be later than when you turned 65 and you will need a SEP (***Special Enrollment Period***) because you are covered under a group health plan based on current employment.

Did You Know that Medicare Provides Hospice at No Cost under Medicare Part A?

Hello Toni:

As a certified case manager and critical care unit RN, I am advising daily adult children who are desperately seeking advice for their parents that are closing in on end of life issues. Those that have serious health care issues should be offered every option for proper planning for end of life care…most appropriately… hospice! I see too many people wait too long to begin hospice benefits

Can you explain hospice for your readers as I am sure this will help those who are seeking answers for their frail loved ones and give the caregiver some well needed rest?

Thanks, in Advance… Susan from Champion Forest area of Houston

Susan

HOSPICE…is a subject no one wants to talk about, let alone be educated about, but can help a family when their loved one is terminally ill and the illness takes a toll on the caregiver and the patient.

This Medicare column's main purpose is to help those that are overwhelmed by a complicated system.

Most believe hospice is for the last days to help a person die peacefully. Many doctors and individuals wait too long to order and receive hospice.

Hospice can give hope along this journey with education, medication to manage symptoms, support to the patient and family, and counseling services for the patient, family members and care givers.

Health care professionals in the hospice system consist of "Special Angels" of physicians, nurses, social workers, spiritual counselors, certified nursing assistants and volunteers. A hospice provider can come to where the patient lives to provide the care and/or much needed relief for the caregiver.

In the Medicare and You Handbook, it explains what hospice is in Medicare terms, and what Medicare covers for hospice under Part A of Medicare. A doctor that orders hospice must certify that you are terminally ill and have 6 (six) months or less to live. (*This does not mean you have to die in 6 months, which is one reason too many caregivers wait to receive care from hospice.)*

Hospice can be recertified every 6 months by a hospice medical director or hospice doctor, if the patient is still terminally ill. Medicare will cover inpatient respite care in a Medicare-approved facility, so that the caregiver can rest. The Hospice patient can stay up to 5 days each time for respite care.

Hospice will cover all medical care for the terminal illness and Medicare will pay for health problems that are not related to your terminal illness (co-pays will apply).

For those who are enrolled in a Medicare Advantage plan, when you are receiving hospice, the hospice benefit will be paid for by Original Medicare, not your Medicare Advantage plan. You will pay your co pay for any medical care that is not associated with the terminal illness

Medicare costs under Hospice:

You pay nothing for hospice care (Medicare pays)
You pay a copayment of up to $5 per prescription for outpatient prescription drugs for pain and symptom management
You pay 5% of the Medicare-approved amount for inpatient respite

You can choose to walk through this journey helpless or have control over your end of life plan of care. Know that hospice provides comfort, dignity, and protection for you and your loved one's wishes with love and support.

Talk with a geriatric case manager or geriatric doctor if you have some concerns or need some advice with your loved one's terminal healthcare issue.

We may not be able to control when we have a terminal illness...But we can control the end of life care ... with understanding hospice.

What is Medicare's 3 Day Skilled Nursing Rule!!

Toni

What is the length of time you have to spend at a hospital before Medicare would pay for a skilled nursing stay. My mother is getting into that situation and we want to make sure Medicare will pay the bill. I would appreciate you refreshing my memory

Thanks, Johnnie - Tampa, FL

Hello Johnnie

Some may have to pay 100% of their skilled nursing and rehabilitative service stay if they do not have enough days **"formally admitted"** in the hospital. The buzz word is **"formally admitted"** for Medicare to pay for the claim. The Medicare "rule" or should I say "qualification" is explained under "Skilled Nursing" in the Medicare and You Handbook.

Review the important information in the Medicare and You Handbook about Skilled Nursing Facility Care

- "Medicare covers semi-private rooms, meals, skilled nursing and rehabilitative service, and other services and supplies that are **medically necessary after a 3-day minimum medically-necessary in-patient hospital stay** for related illness or injury. An in-patient hospital stay begins the day you're formally admitted with a doctor's order and doesn't include the day you are discharged."

Toni Says® *Make sure you are formally admitted for at least 4 days... the 3-day hospital stay plus 1 day for being discharged*

- "To qualify for care in a skilled nursing facility, your doctor must certify that you need daily skilled care like intravenous injections or physical therapy."

Many are not **"formally admitted"** into the hospital because of the new "2-day observation rule" until their doctor has finished all of the testing, MRIs, scans...etc., and knows what type of medical care or surgery is needed. Until there has been a diagnosis, a person is generally "in observation" and has not been **"formally admitted."**

The average person does not know the hospital's protocol or language, so how would they know the difference between observation or formally admitted. Maybe reality TV should do a TV showon understanding this situation since "the skilled nursing 3-day rule" affects so many unsuspecting Americans who are using Medicare every day.

This situation happened to my husband's father who was hospitalized after he broke his hip on Monday. He had surgery performed Wednesday which was the day he was considered **"formally admitted."** He was moved to a skilled facility 2 days later, on that Friday. Because he was not **"formally admitted"** in the hospital for "3 midnight stays" and discharged the next day, he was sent a bill for 100% of the skilled nursing facility bill because of this rule.

✍ ***Note*** - Remember the rule says you must stay 3 days past midnight after being formally admitted to qualify.

When someone is seriously ill and family members are trying to juggle everyday life, you would think that there would be a person at the hospital with the job of making sure that people do not get caught in this situation. Case managers are overloaded just keeping up with the new Medicare rules and guidelines because of healthcare reform

Medicare would say you are sent the Medicare and You Handbook therefore they have notified everyone. Many skilled nursing facilities do not realize that there is a "3 midnight stay" rule problem until after their client has either been in their facility for a few days or has been discharged to go home and they have billed Medicare.

Toni Says® Please review the article titled "Will the Medicare Observation Rule Affect You?" This changed stays as an in-patient in the hospital trying to control the cost of skilled nursing in a hospital stay. The MOON rule has made the stay in the hospital longer to qualify for Medicare to pay for Skilled Nursing. There is still a "3 midnight stay" rule to qualify for Medicare to pay for Skilled Nursing care but you also have the 2-day MOON (observation rule). At the time of writing the new Medicare Survival Guide® Advanced edition, there is nothing in the Medicare and You Handbook about the March 8, 2017 Medicare change. You can contact the Toni Says® team of professions at **info@tonisays.com** for more information. We will stay abreast of these changes and inform our readers as updates are finalized.

Medicare Stopped Paying My Husband's Skilled Nursing
Must Pay $4000/month or Take Him Home!!

Toni

My husband is 67 years old and suffered a severe stroke this January; his skilled/rehab facility is saying Medicare will not pay for his care anymore. I've been informed that beginning next week to receive care from this facility, it will have to be either private pay of about $4000 or I will have to take him home

He is over 6 feet tall and weighs 275 lbs. I cannot lift him and have a full-time job which I cannot quit, since I am the only one working. There is no family close by, what can I do! I thought Medicare paid for your care when you are sick. I need some help trying to understand this confusing system. What is the difference in rehab/skilled care and long-term care? I thought they were both the same!!

Elizabeth from Katy, TX

Elizabeth

Situations like yours are the reason I do the "Confused about Medicare" workshops and wrote the Medicare Survival Guide® because your health can change drastically in the blink of an eye and you must be prepared when life throws you a curve!

It is very frustrating to understand the rules of Medicare when a loved one has a severe illness and requires both medical and custodial care. I will try and explain the difference of rehab/skilled nursing and long-term care in as simple terms as I can.

Medicare only pays for medically-necessary rehab/skilled nursing facility care, if you meet certain medical conditions and criteria. Rehab/skilled nursing has only100 days of benefit with days 1-20 being a $0 co-pay per day and days 21-100 with a specific co-pay per day which changes every year. If you cannot qualify or do not meet Medicare's qualification for rehab/skilled nursing, you will pay 100% of the cost out of your pocket as you are experiencing right now. Your husband either has met the maximum day amount or he does not meet the medical qualifications for improving his health condition for rehab/skilled nursing. This is where Long-Term Care and purchasing a Long-Term Care policy becomes so important.

Long-Term Care includes medical and non-medical care for people who have a chronic illness or disability. They may need help with activities of daily living such as bathing, dressing, eating, transferring, continence, ability to use the bathroom or cognitive impairment. At least 70% of people over 65 will need long-term care services at some point. Long-term care can be provided at home, in an adult day care, an assisted living facility, personal care home or in a nursing ho

Long-term care can be costly with the average cost ranging from $40,000 a year for a 1 bedroom assisted living facility to $65,000 a year for an average nursing home room.

There are many different ways to help pay for long-term care.

. Purchase a long-term care policy. The younger you are, the lower the premiums will be. My advice is to consider a Long-Term Care policy while you are younger and in relatively good health. Make sure that your policy covers care at home and facility care.
2. Use your personal resources such as savings, IRA, 401K etc. Many life policies have a provision for if you need long-term care; you can receive a certain amount of your life policy's face amount
3. Check to see if you can qualify for Medicaid. Many have to "spend down" to qualify. See the <u>Medicare and You Handbook</u> for more information on Medicaid and Long-Term Care.
4. Aid and Attendant benefits with the VA can help Veterans with Long-term Care issues.
5. Reverse mortgage is another option. Talk to your banker about that option.

Helping my In-Laws with Long-Term Care Issues at Home?

Dear Toni

I desperately need your help regarding my husband's parents who are in their late 80s. My mother-in-law has been very sick for the past 3 years and my father-in-law has been her caretaker. I've always heard that the one, who becomes the caretaker, also becomes the one who needs additional medical care. He has never been a sick person, but now he cannot help her. He has lost almost 50 pounds over the past year and has just been released from the hospital because he was so dehydrated and lost so much weight so fast

They do not have a long-term care plan. Talking about live-in help or even talking about an Assisted Living facility is out of the question. Their big worry is that they will outlive their retirement money and believe they can take care of themselves

My husband and my worry is that we know they cannot properly take care of themselves and since my father-in-law is still driving he may have a wreck and kill someone

Can you help us explore some options that are out there that can help relieve some of this burden?

Sandy in Sugar Land, TX

Hi Sandy:

Don't feel like you are alone because many baby-boomers are experiencing just what you are facing. Elderly parents can be quite trying because they do not want to lose their independence. It is so difficult when you know they need extra help. Many in this age bracket do not have a Long-Term Care Policy and are very conservative when it comes to spending extra money.

My husband and I have experienced the problem. We talked with a home health agency who explained how his parents could maximize their Medicare dollars with home healthcare benefits. There is not a co-pay or deductible for home healthcare. "Original" Medicare will pay 100% for any medical services provided by a home healthcare agency.

Those on "Original" Medicare have "Patient's Rights" and they have the "right" to choose which home healthcare agency they want to use. Those who are enrolled in a Medicare Advantage plan must use network providers and may be limited to how much home healthcare one can receive. Be sure which way your husband's parents are receiving their Medicare benefit

To receive home health care services from Medicare

. There must be a medical need to receive home health services
2. The Doctor must order the home healthcare services
3. You must need intermittent skilled nursing care, physical, speech or occupational therapy.
4. The home health agency must be certified by Medicare.
5. You must be homebound. Homebound means that leaving home takes considerable and taxing effort. Someone can be homebound and still go to the beauty shop or go to church.

Once these conditions are met, Original Medicare will cover the types of care listed below:

- Skilled nursing care which can only be performed by a licensed
- Home health aide that can assist in bathing, dressing and other personal care that must be part of the health care for the illness or injury.
- Physical, speech or occupational therapy can be ordered.
- Medical social worker can help with long-term planning and help find resources
- Certain medical supplies such as wound dressing, catheters, colostomies (but not prescriptions drug).
- Durable medical equipment such as wheelchair, walker, crutches, hospital bed.

Consult with your loved one's primary care or specialist, if you believe home healthcare might be right for your loved ones. Most generally, your Physician, a Social Worker, Case Manager, or a Hospital Discharge Planner can help arrange for Medicare-covered home healthcare

ToniSays.com **Toni Says®** Remember, you have "PATIENT'S RIGHTS", and this gives you a say in which home health agency you want to use.

Medicare Part B (Medical Coverage)

Why did Enrolling in Medicare Part B while Working with Company Benefits Cost Me $5,000?

Dear Toni

When I turned 65 I was told by friends to enroll in Part B to keep from getting the dreaded Part B penalty, even though I had great company benefits with the company that I had worked for 30 years. Now I would like to pick a Medicare Supplement/medigap Policy, but finding out I cannot get any plan I want like my other co-workers, who are way past 65 and are now receiving their Medicare Part B

I would like to apply for a Medicare Supplement Plan G and because I've had Part B in place, I can't due to heart surgery I had 2 years ago. I now should answer health questions due to the fact that I don't qualify for Medicare Supplement Open enrollment. I've paid $5,000 for Medicare Part B when I could have waited

Please explain what I need to do to get Medicare Supplement/medigap coverage for both me and my wife? We need your help

Thanks, Bob from New York, NY

Hello Bob

Every day I talk to someone who gets the wrong information from a well-meaning friend. As I have said before, Medicare provides special rules for those who are "still working" with true company benefits

In the Medicare and You Handbook, it explains how to enroll in Medicare and what to do when leaving your company benefits after 65. The Medicare and You Handbook states,

> *When you sign up for Part* B, your Medicare Supplement/Medigap Open Enrollment Period begins."

Bob, you are past your Medicare Supplement/Medigap Open Enrollment Period. In the Medicare and You Handbook, it states, The best time to buy a Medicare Supplement/Medigap policy is during your Medicare Supplement/Medigap Open Enrollment Period. This 6-month period begins on the first day of the month in which you're 65 or older **and** enrolled in Part B. (Some states have additional Open Enrollment Periods.) After this enrollment period, you may not be able to buy a Medicare Supplement/ Medigap policy. If you're able to buy one it may cost more."

Therefore enrolling in Part B the correct way, when "still working" full-time with true company benefits is so important. Not only to keep from receiving a Medicare Part B penalty, but also to be able to enroll and be accepted in any Medicare Supplement/Medigap pl

Your saving grace is that you are being terminated from you or your spouse's company benefits and can receive a 63-day guaranteed issue period for applying for a Medicare Supplement/Medigap plan. Keep your company benefit termination letter to show the Medicare Supplement insurance company that you are in a guarantee issue period.

With guaranteed issue rights, an insurance company must:

Sell you a Medicare Supplement/Medigap policy. "You have the right to buy Medicare Supplement/ Medigap plan A, B, C, F, K or L that's sold in your state by any insurance company

- Cover all your pre-existing health conditions.

Cannot charge you more for a Medicare Supplement/Medigap policy, regardless of past or present health problems.

No one realizes the value to first receiving Part B until they are in your situation and now they want to apply for a Medicare Supplement/Medigap and can only get certain plans because they are no longer in their Open Enrollment Period.

Does Medicare Cover Cataract Surgery?

Toni

I will be eligible for Medicare soon and I'm trying to compare Medicare to my current company benefits? I am concerned that if I need cataracts removed, this procedure will not be covered with Medicare

I can take my company dental and vision benefits when I retire and am wondering if that is a good idea or are dental/vision benefits available with Medicare?

Tim from Arlington, TX

Hello…Tim

Medicare covers many medically necessary surgical procedures and cataract surgery is covered. In the Medicare and You Handbook, under eyeglasses it will explain about cataract coverage.

If you're having surgery or a procedure, you can do some things in advance to figure out approximately how much you'll have to pay.

- Ask the doctor, hospital, or facility how much you'll have to pay for the surgery and any care afterward

Make sure you know if you're an "in-patient or outpatient" because what you pay may be different. Check with other insurance you may have (like a Medicare Supplement/medigap Insurance policy, Medicaid, or coverage from your or your spouse's employer) to see what it will pay. If you belong to a Medicare Advantage plan, contact your plan for more information and how they will pay.

In the Medicare and You Handbook, under "What's NOT Covered by Part A & Part B" it states

> *"Medicare does not cover everything and if you need certain services that Medicare doesn't cover, you will have to pay for them yourself unless you have other insurance to cover the costs."*

The Medicare and You Handbook also states

> *You may have other insurance (including Medicaid) that could cover the costs*
> *You may be in a Medicare health plan such as Medicare Advantage (Part C) that may cover these services*

✍*<u>**Note**</u> Remember, if Medicare covers a service, then you generally must pay deductibles, coinsurances, and co-pays.

What Medicare does not cover?

Long-term care, routine dental care, dentures, cosmetic surgery, acupuncture, hearing aids including exams for fitting hearing aids are not covered.

Since Medicare doesn't cover dental, I would recommend that you talk to your dentist and see which dental insurance plan he/she prefers.

The Medicare handbook, talks about eyeglasses, which is a limited benefit because Medicare will cover one pair of eyeglasses with standard frames (or one set of contact lenses) <u>after</u> cataract surgery that implants an intraocular lens. The Medicare Part B deductible will apply and you will pay the 20% of the Medicare-approved amount.

Hearing aids are also considered elective, just like glasses. Medicare covers the exams if your doctor or other health care provider orders them. Again, you pay the 20% of the Medicare-approved amount and the Part B deductible applies. Medicare does not cover the hearing aids or exams for fitting the hearing aids and this can be expensive.

"Quite honestly, they don't care if a person can see, hear or have teeth to eat with. If you can't afford dentures, you're going to have to gum your food to death!" That quote comes from my husband.

If you can keep these ancillary benefits when you retire, it may be a good idea. Group benefit plans are generally more comprehensive.

Medicare Rules Changed July 1, 2013 regarding Medical Equipment

Reader Alert: New Medicare Rules took Effect July 1, 2013 for Mail Order Diabetic Supplies and Various Medical Equipment such as Oxygen, C-PAP, wheel chair etc. Please read below

Dear Toni

I am diabetic and need help!! I order my diabetic test strips from a mail-order program and they are delivered to my front door. Toni, I received a letter stating my supplier will no longer be covered by Medicare because it is not a "competitive bidding" supplier. Does this mean that if I continue with my current supplier, Medicare will stop paying for my diabetic test strips? What is going on?

Sandra from Memorial area

Hello Sandra

Beginning July 1, 2013, Medicare started new rules about mail-order diabetic supplies, such as test strips and lancets. And this is confusing a lot of folks!!

If Medicare is your primary insurance, *you use only "Original" Medicare Parts A and B (this does not affect a Part C Medicare Advantage plan)* and you order your supplies from a mail-order supplier, you must use suppliers who have been awarded a contract under a new "competitive bidding" rule or you will have to pay 100% out of your pocket. Confusing, I know.

Medicare has a listing of these approved suppliers; the list is available either online at **www.medicare.gov** or by calling 1-800-Medicare.

The new mail-order program does not require you to change the particular testing monitor, test strips and lancets you currently are using. Remember, Medicare only wants you to use the mail-order supplier that they approve. If you are happy with the monitor, test strips and lancets you are currently using, you will want to use a competitive bidding supplier that stocks your testing items. You will needto provide your new supplier with either a new prescription for your diabetic supplies or have your current prescription transferred. Talk to your doctor about a new prescription, it's probably going tobe easier

If you would rather, you could opt to discontinue home delivery of your diabetic supplies and purchase your diabetic supplies at a local pharmacy (that is enrolled in Medicare). This way, "Original Medicare" Part B will provide the diabetic supplies and you have to pay the 20% co-pay or your Medicare Supplement/medigap or retirement insurance can pick up the 20%. If you have more questions about the changes in Medicare's policy, contact Medicare at 1-800-Medicare or talk to your pharmacy. I am sure the pharmacies are being bombarded with questions.

Here is another Medicare change which began July 1st concerning Durable Medical Equipmentsent to your house, such as wheel chairs, walkers, oxygen, CPAP devices, at home wound equipment orany type of medical device you use at home.

Medicare will only cover a Durable Medical Equipment or at-home supplier in your area that have either a competitive bidding status or has been "grandfathered". What is "grandfathered"? A "grandfathered" supplier simply means Medicare will continue to cover the supplier's current customers for a "limited" period of time.

If your supplier has been granted a "grandfathered" status, you may continue to use this medical supplier after July 1, 2013. BUT!! At some time in the future, you will need to switch to a competitive bidder of medical equipment.

***Note** - Remember to confirm with your "grandfathered" medical supplier, the time length you may continue to use that particular supplier under Medicare's new rules

Reader Alert: Once the "grandfathered" time limit has expired, you will need to use a competitive bidding medical supplier or you may have to pay 100% out of your pocket.

Toni Says® Be sure you are using a competitive bidding medical supplier when receiving your medical equipment at home or you might have to pay 100% out of your pocket!!

Does Medicare Pay for Allergy Shots?

Toni

I am turning 65 this October and currently am enrolled in a Blue Cross/Blue Shield $4,000 deductible individual health insurance plan. My biggest medical expense is from shots that I receive from 2 doctors

One is allergy shots taken 3 times a week from my allergist. One of the shots is not very expensive, but the shot for macular degeneration is over $2,000 per shot. It does not take me too many months or treatments for me to make the $4,000 deductible

My concern is what or how does Medicare Part B pay for these 2 medical procedures? Look forward to your answer

Sharon, Edmond, OK

Great question, Sharon:

Most Americans do not realize what is covered under Medicare Part B which is the medical insurance part of Medicare.

The Medicare and You Handbook, discusses "What does Part B cover?" It states that Part B "helps to cover medically necessary doctors' services, outpatient care, home health services, durable medical equipment and other medical services.

Many preventative services that are covered under Part B are listed in the Medicare and You Handbook

Sharon, you mentioned that you have a concern about whether expensive macular degeneration shot for your eye and also the allergy testing and shots can be covered under Medicare Part B. As long as these procedures are medically necessary, then Medicare will pay for those procedures.

"Medically necessary" as defined by Medicare means:

> *"health-care services or supplies needed to prevent, diagnose, or treat an illness, injury, condition, disease, or its symptoms and that meet accepted standards of medicine."*

The Medicare and You Handbook also says under "Doctor and other health care provider services" that

"Medicare covers medically necessary doctor services (including outpatient services and some doctor services you get when you're a hospital in-patient), and covered preventative services. Medicare covers other health care providers like physician assistants, nurse practitioners, social workers, physical therapists and psychologists."

The Part B medical/doctor deductible changes each year, with Medicare paying 80% of theMedicare approved amount and you (the Medicare beneficiary) paying 20% of the Medicare approved amount

To help pay for the 20% out of pocket, many enrolled in Medicare chose a Medicare Supplement/ Medigap Policy to help defray the Medicare Parts A and B deductibles and out of pocket charges. With a Medicare Supplement/Medigap, Sharon, you will have low or no out of pocket for Medicare medically necessary approved amounts depending on which Medicare Supplement/Medigap plan you are enrolled

The Medicare and You Handbook states that "if you're in a Medicare Advantage Plan (like a HMO or PPO) or have other insurance, your costs may be different. Contact your plan or benefits administrator to find out the costs."

Part B has a monthly premium and for those new to Medicare who enrolled in Part B, the premium may change each year. Some on Medicare with income more than $85,001.00 for an individual or $170,001.00 for a couple, will pay more each month for their Medicare Part B

Does Medicare Pay for Diabetic Supplies?

Dear Toni

I am diabetic and I order my diabetic test strips from a mail-order program through my company benefits which are delivered to my front door. Recently, I have been laid off and am enrolling in Medicare

How do I receive my diabetic supplies since I am new to Medicare?

Toni, I received a letter stating my supplier will no longer be covered by Medicare because it is not a "competitive bidding" supplier. Does this mean that if I continue with my current supplier, Medicare will stop paying for my diabetic test strips? Please explain

Silvia, Memphis, TN

Hello Silvia

Beginning July 1, 2013, Medicare began new rules about mail-order diabetic supplies, such as test strips, monitors, lancets etc. And this has confused a lot of folks.

If Medicare is your primary insurance, *you use only "Original" Medicare Parts A and B with a Medicare Supplement (Medicare Advantage Part C plans have different rules)* and you order your supplies from a mail-order supplier, you must use suppliers who have been awarded a contract under a new "competitive bidding" rules or you will have to pay 100% out of your pocket. This process is only for mail order diabetic or medical supplies.

Medicare has a listing of approved mail order and local suppliers; the list is available either online at **www.medicare.gov** or by calling 1-800-Medicare (633-4227).

The mail-order program does not require you to change the particular testing monitor, test strips and lancets you currently are using. Remember, Medicare only wants you to use the mail-order supplier that Medicare approves. If you are happy with the monitor, test strips and lancets you are currently using, you will want to use a competitive bidding supplier that stocks your testing items. You will need to provide your new supplier with either a new prescription for your diabetic supplies or have your current prescription transferred.

You need a new prescription from your doctor for your lancets and test strips every 12 months. Very important because if you do not receive a new prescription, you will pay 100% out of your own pocket.

If you would rather, you could change from home delivery of your diabetic supplies and purchase your diabetic supplies at a local pharmacy (that is a Medicare provider).

"Original Medicare" Part B will provide the diabetic supplies and you must pay the 20% co pay or your Medicare Supplement can pick up the 20%. If you have more questions about the changes in Medicare's policy, contact Medicare at 1-800-Medicare or talk to your pharmacy.

Many on Medicare are concerned about durable medical equipment (DME) that is sent to your house or that you use on a day by day basis, such as wheel chairs, walkers, oxygen, CPAP devices, at home wound equipment or any medical device you use at home.

Medicare will only cover a durable medical equipment or at-home supplier in your area that has a competitive bidding status.

You should also make sure that the pharmacy or medical supplier accepts assignment for Medicare-covered supplies. Assignment is an agreement between you (the person with Medicare), Medicare, and doctors, other health care suppliers, or providers. If the pharmacy or supplier accepts assignment, Medicare will pay the pharmacy or supplier directly. You only pay your coinsurance amount when you get your supply from a pharmacy or supplier for assigned claims

Always ask:

- Are you enrolled in Medicare?
- Do you accept Medicare assignment?

Why Prescriptions Cost More to those on Medicare in ER or Outpatient Facilities which is Under Medicare Part B?

Dear Toni

I have been told that Medicare does not cover drugs when you are in an emergency room? My mother went in the hospital from the ER for 2 days and because it was considered "under observation," we are now fighting the hospital because they say her drugs were not covered during her stay. She has a Part D plan but the claim is filed out of network and she has to pay a higher amount, she used her Part D plan. We do not know what to do or if we can be reimbursed from her Part D Medicare Plan? Please explain what her options are?

Thanks, Sydnie from Lake Jackson

Hello Sydnie,

If you are not enrolled in a Medicare Prescription Drug Part D plan and your hospital stay falls in "under observation" you may pay for the drugs administered because your stay is under Part B which does not cover prescriptions given orally. Part B (Medical Insurance) covers IV (intravenous infusion) drugs and since your mother was considered outpatient care she was not an inpatient care, which would have qualified her for a Medicare Part D, an inpatient hospital stay.

Medicare Part B generally covers care that you receive in a hospital outpatient setting like an emergency room, observation unit, and outpatient surgery center or pain clinic.

This is why enrolling in a Part D Medicare drug plan is so important because when you are admitted in a hospital on an outpatient basis you may need your self-administered drugs. Self-administered drugs are what you would normally take on your own or over the counter type drugs. Part B does not pay for these types of drugs, but a Medicare Part D Prescription Drug plan can

If you do not have a Part D drug plan while in a Part B "under observation," hospital outpatient setting or emergency room, then you may pay for the drug cost out of your pocket.

When I am consulting with someone who is first enrolling in Medicare and they try to justify why they do not need to enroll in a Part D drug plan when they do not take any prescriptions; I simply advise them how important it is to enroll in the least expensive Part D plan.

No one knows what the future holds and now with healthcare reform; Medicare is doing everything they can to control how they are spending "our" Medicare dollar

New Medicare rules are popping up each month to make sure Medicare dollars are being spent wisely.

To keep from paying for prescriptions out of pocket when in the hospital, I would advise you to get your mother enrolled in a Part D plan when Medicare's open enrollment takes place on October 15 to December 7

Below is what to do when you receive a hospital bill for prescriptions not covered by Part B in a hospital outpatient setting:

- Most hospital pharmacies do not participate in Medicare Part D; you may need to pay up front and submit the claim to your Medicare drug plan for a refund.
- Follow instructions on how to submit an out-of-network claim
- You may need to forward certain information like emergency room bills that show what self-administered drugs you were given.
- You might need to explain the reason for the hospital visit.
- Keep copies of receipts and paper work you send to your Part D plan.

Research about Part B outpatient hospital setting and Part D was found on the Medicare website at **http://www.medicare.gov/Pubs/pdf/11333.pdf**

Concerns are Rising about Doctors Not Accepting or Billing Medicare

Hi Toni

This week, I went to see a neurologist and his office said that since Medicare is primary on my insurance, I would have to pay upfront the complete bill and be reimbursed by Medicare. His office is a small office and the paperwork is killing him. Also, he will be retiring soon, so I need to find a new neurologist

Can you please tell me what I need to do to submit this doctor visit and get reimbursed?

Thank you so much –Susan…Spring, TX

Hello Susan

In these trying healthcare times that we are in because of healthcare reform, some of the smaller medical providers whether a primary care or a specialist are opting out of the Medicare system.

They are not accepting Medicare as your doctor is doing and will not bill Medicare for you either. They want you to submit the bill to Medicare and wait to be reimbursed

Did the doctor charge Medicare rates or charge you their rates and want you to be reimbursed from Medicare what Medicare will pay? That is what it sounds like to

I am hearing through the Medicare grapevine from clients that come in the Toni Says® office for a Medicare consultation that many of the older primary care and medical providers are retiring because the office paperwork whether it is for Medicare or under 65 medical claims is very overwhelming. My advice to clients who are new to Medicare to begin searching for medical providers, especially when a serious health issue is involved

I have not heard of this type of problem with larger medical offices, especially those who are part of a hospital system.

Below are a few tips that I tell my clients which can help you.

1) Before you set the appointment for your medical visit, ask the doctor's office, if they are still accepting Medicare. Most important, that they are accepting new Medicare patients and will that office bill Medicare directly.
2) If they say NO, then you need to decide…Do I want to pay out of pocket and get reimbursed what Medicare pays. Doctors know they are not paid their asking rates. Medicare is not the only one who discounts the doctor's bills. Group and individual health insurance plans with network providers, also discounts the doctor's bills…. OR…
3) Look for a doctor or specialist that does take Medicare assignment and will bill Medicare. There are plenty doctors and healthcare professionals that still accept and bill Medicare and are accepting new Medicare patients. Even top in their specific medical field specialists still take Medicare. Ask your primary care doctor for more than one doctor or provider that he/she recommends for your specific medical situation.

Here is how to file a claim if your doctor doesn't accept Medicare assignment. You may have to pay the complete bill and submit the claim to Medicare. Look in the Medicare and You Handbook, which explains how to submit a claim. You need to call 1/800-MEDICARE (633-4227) and ask for Form CMS-1490S or go to **www.medicare.gov/medicareonlineforms**. When you have Medicare on the phone, ask them for help with filing the claim and they will be happy to assist. Good Luck, Susan

Doctor's New Rule…Pay Up Front and YOU…File with Medicare!!

Hi Toni

I have Original Medicare and a Medicare Supplement Plan F. No problem in the past filing with Medicare, but beginning January 1st, my neurologist has changed how he bills Medicare. As a small office, he said that because of the amount of paperwork, he no longer files with Medicare

I would have to pay up front and be reimbursed by Medicare. Can you please tell me what I need to do to submit this visit for reimbursement? Could this be the beginning of doctor problems because of Obamacare?

Thank you so much –Susan … Dallas, Texas

Hello Susan

This year's Medicare's Annual Enrollment Period (aka Open Enrollment) has a completely different "environment" because many of the Medicare beneficiaries are concerned they are going to lose their doctors if they have Original Medicare with a supplement or many that are members of a Medicare Advantage plan were informed that their doctors or specialists were no longer part of that specific Medicare Advantage plan.

People really do not like change, especially when it comes to their healthcare and the doctor, who they have faith in.

In these trying economic times that we are in and with all of the changes with Medicare, as you are experiencing, many doctors are not accepting Medicare and will not bill Medicare for you. They want you to submit the bill to Medicare and wait to be reimbursed.

Does your neurologist or any specialist charge Medicare rates or did the doctor's office charge you their rates and want you to be reimbursed from Medicare what Medicare rate will be? That is what it sounds like to me. And who knows how long it takes for Medicare to reimburse you.

Here are a few tips that I tell my clients which can help you when having this problem:

1. Before you set the appointment ask the doctor's office if they accept **Medicare assignment** and will bill Medicare directly for you. (This will be your easiest way)
2. If they say **NO,** then you need to decide, do I want to pay out of pocket and get reimbursed what Medicare pays? Doctors know they are not paid their asking rates. Medicare is not the only one who discounts the doctor's bills. Group health insurance also discounts the doctor's bills. OR
3. Look for a doctor/specialist that takes **Medicare assignment** and will bill Medicare. There are plenty of fantastic doctors/specialist that do accept Medicare. More doctors and specialists are taking Medicare than those that don't. Ask your primary care doctor/specialist for more than one doctor or specialist that he/she can refer for you.

Toni's Tip on how to file a Medicare claim

Here is how to file a claim if your doctor doesn't accept Medicare assignment. You may have to pay the complete bill and submit the claim to Medicare. See "What is assignment?" in the Medicare and You Handbook which explains how to submit a claim if your doctor, provider, or supplier doesn't accept assignment. You can call 1/800-MEDICARE (633-4227) and ask for Form CMS-1490S or go to **medicare.gov/medicareonlineforms**

When you have Medicare on the phone, ask them for help with filing the claim and they will be happy to assist

Moving Overseas...Should I Keep My Medicare?

Hello, Toni:

My husband and I are currently on Medicare with Part B, a supplement, and Part D coverage. We will be moving overseas for a couple of years. I know that there is no coverage from Medicare for overseas expenses

Is there a way to suspend our Medicare coverage (and the supplements & Part D) while we are overseas and reinstate it without a penalty when we return? It's a large expense to have to pay premiums in both countries, but only to have benefit from one. If we were to drop the supplement and Part D while we are gone, would we have to be underwritten if we return (i.e. excluded if we have pre-existing conditions)?

Thanks for your help with this. Part of our planning is trying to figure out our expenses while we are out of the country

Thank You...Sandy, Houston, TX

Good-day, Sandy:

That's a great question. Will you or your husband be working full time with true company benefits? Or are you just moving out of the country for a few years to get away?

If you or your husband will be working with company benefits, then you can delay Part B until you return to the States without getting the "famous" Medicare Part B penalty.

If not working full-time with company benefits, then I would advise you and your husband to remain enrolled in Medicare and keep your Medicare Supplemental plan because no one ever knows what will happen to your health in the future.

If you decide to drop your Medicare Supplement/Medigap and return to the United States later, you will be subject to underwriting and have to answer health questions to re-enroll into a new Medicare Supplement/Medigap for both you and your husband.

Yours is not the first question that I have received about stopping one's Medicare Part B when moving overseas and then you have a serious health issue. You then want to return to the US and re-enroll in Medicare Part B only to discover that your Medicare Part B penalty will go all the way back to the day you turned 65 at a 10% penalty for each year to when you were 65.

Let's say you and your spouse are 75 years old when you return to the States and re-enroll in Medicare. You and your spouse's Medicare Part B penalty will be 75-65=10 years times 10% or 100% penalty. Not for one month, but for the rest of you and your spouse's Medicare enrollment

Not only will you have a Medicare penalty, but you will also have a Medicare Part D penalty because you let your Part D prescription drug plan expire. The only way to keep from having a Part D penalty is to have been enrolled in any type of creditable prescription drug coverage such as company benefits or VA prescription drug plan.

ToniSays.com **Toni Says®** When you do not enroll in Medicare Part B or you decide to cancel your Part B because you are moving out of the country and want to re-enroll at a later date, you will have the famous Part B penalty which will go back to the day you turned 65. Remember Medicare does not have any do-over rules

Chapter 3

Medicare Supplement or Medigap Policies

(Same thing, different names)

Medicare Supplement or Medigap Policies

Medicare Supplement FREEDOM of CHOICE!

- You must have Part **A** and Part **B**
- Enroll at the right time to get ***Guaranteed Issue!***
- Works only with Original Medicare (your Red, White and Blue Card)
- The cost goes up each year!
- **A supplement does not have Part D** Medicare Prescription Drug Plan
- May Enroll in a Medicare Prescription Drug Plan to avoid Part D penalties

Original/Traditional Medicare has more holes than SWISS CHEESE! My advice to you, if you are searching for a Medicare insurance plan to pick up out of pocket expenses that Original/ Traditional Medicare does not pay for, is to search for a Medicare Supplement/Medigap. With Original/Traditional Medicare, there is not a network of providers or facilities that you must choose from to receive medical care. Be sure to ask your provider or facility if they are accepting Original or Traditional Medicare. The down side is the cost. The cost will go up each year with yearly policy rate increases.

Medicare DOES NOT pay any of the costs for a Medicare Supplement/Medigap policy *(which is what Medicare calls it and most people know it as Medicare supplement)* You must pay the premiums out of your pocket

You must be enrolled in both Medicare Parts A & B to enroll in a Medicare Supplement/ Medigap policy.

In the Medicare and You Handbook, it states, "A Medicare Supplement/Medigap policy is a private health insurance that helps supplement Original/Traditional Medicare."

A Medicare Supplement/Medigap policy works with Original Medicare (*which is Part A and Part B listed on your red, white and blue Medicare card*) and you cannot use a Medicare Supplement/Medigap to pay your co pays, or deductibles for *"Part C" Medicare Advantage Plans*

If an insurance agent knows that you are already enrolled in a Medicare Advantage plan, then they cannot enroll you in a Medicare Supplement/Medigap policy.

A Medicare Supplement/Medigap policy must be clearly identified as "Medicare Supplemental Insurance" because it supplements what Medicare does not pay. Every insurance company can only sell what is called a "Standardized" Medigap policies, which are identified by letters A-D, F, G, K, L, M and N. The Medicare and You Handbook also states, "All Medigap policies must follow federal and state laws designed to protect you.

OUTLINE OF MEDICARE SUPPLEMENT COVERAGE – COVER PAGE
BENEFIT PLANS A, F, G, HIGH DEDUCTIBLE G AND N
Benefit Chart of Medicare Supplement Plans Sold on or after January 1, 2020

This chart shows the benefits included in each of the standard Medicare supplement plans. Every company must make Plan A available. Some plans may not be available. Only applicants **first** eligible for Medicare before 2020 may purchase Plans C, F and High Deductible F.

Note: A ✓ means 100% of the benefit is paid.

Benefits	Plans Available to All Applicants (High Deductible G not available prior to July 1, 2019 with an Effective Date – January 1, 2020 or later.)								Medicare first eligible before 2020 only	
	A	B	D	G / G[1]	K	L	M	N	C	F / F[1]
Medicare Part A coinsurance and hospital coverage (up to an additional 365 days after Medicare benefits are used up)	✓	✓	✓	✓	✓	✓	✓	✓	✓	✓
Medicare Part B coinsurance or Copayment	✓	✓	✓	✓	50%	75%	✓	✓ copays apply[3]	✓	✓
Blood (first three pints each year)	✓	✓	✓	✓	50%	75%	✓	✓	✓	✓
Part A hospice care coinsurance or copayment	✓	✓	✓	✓	50%	75%	✓	✓	✓	✓
Skilled nursing facility coinsurance			✓	✓	50%	75%	✓	✓	✓	✓
Medicare Part A deductible		✓	✓	✓	50%	75%	50%	✓	✓	✓
Medicare Part B deductible									✓	✓
Medicare Part B excess charges				✓						✓
Foreign travel emergency (up to plan limits)			✓	✓			✓	✓	✓	✓
Out-of-pocket limit in 2020[2]					$5,880[2]	$2,940[2]				

In the Medicare and You Handbook, it states when is the best time to buy a Medicare Supplement/ Medigap policy without having to answer any health questions. This special time period is called your Medigap Open Enrollment Period. The period lasts for 6 months and begins on the first day of the month when you are both 65 or older and have enrolled in Medicare Part B. More specifics about Medigap Open Enrollment Period in the articles at the end of the chapter.

Four ways to receive your Medicare Supplement/Medigap when enrolling in Medicare or leaving company benefits are below:

1) **Turning 65 and enrolling in Medicare Part B**, you will have Medigap/Medicare Supplement Open Enrollment Period last for a 6-month period and begins the first day that you are 65 and enrolled in Part B. You can enroll in whichever Medicare Supplement/ Medigap plan you select in the above chart. No prescription drug coverage included.
2) **Past 65 and enrolling in Medicare Part B,** you and your spouse, that may also be past 65, will have the same 6-month period which begins the first day of the month that you or our spouse are enrolled in Part B. You can enroll in whichever Medigap/Medicare Supplement Plan you select in the above chart. No prescription drug coverage included.

3) **63 Day guaranteed issue period NOT 6 months**, as in items #1 and #2, is for those who have had Medicare Part B in place longer than 6 months but is either retiring with company benefits or already retired and leaving retiree benefits or COBRA benefits. Only specific Medicare Supplement/Medigap plans A, B, C, F, K or L are available to those enrolled in Medicare Part A which started prior to January 1, 2020 can be sold in your state by any insurance company. Those with Medicare Part A which begins after January 1, 2020 qualify for Medicare Plan G with Plan C and F is no longer available to those with Medicare Part A effective date after January 1, 2020. You will have 63 days from when coverage ends, and you must have a termination notice from the insurance company stating the date that you or your spouse's coverage is ending. No prescription drug coverage included.
4) **63 Day guaranteed issue period** when your Medicare Supplement/Medigap plan or Medicare Advantage plan is no longer participating in the Medicare program and has sent you a letter stating they will no longer be covering you. 63 days of guaranteed issue begins the day that you or your spouse's coverage ends. During this time, your health conditions cannot keep you from receiving certain Medicare Supplement/Medigap plans A, B, C, F, K, or L available to those who Medicare Part A begins prior to January 1, 2020 and after January 1, 2020 those qualify for Medicare Plan G with Plan C and F no longer available to those with Medicare Part A effective date is after January 1, 2020. Your Medicare Supplement/ Medigap policy or Medicare Advantage plan must be leaving your area to qualify. No prescription drug coverage included.

✍ ***Note**: Not paying or terminating your coverage does not qualify you for a guarantee issue period.

When you apply for a Medicare Supplement/Medigap policy, there is not a Medicare Prescription Drug Part D plan attached You will need to apply for Part D when applying for the Medicare Supplement/ Medigap policy. Please visit www.medicare.gov and click on "find health and drug plans." Place all your prescriptions in the system and it will inform you which plans best meet your needs.

Search through the table of contents for your specific Medicare Supplement/Medigap questions or read the rest of this chapter and gain Medicare Supplement/Medigap knowledge to help your friends that are confused. Below are articles from the Toni Says newspaper column regarding specific questions concerning Medicare Supplements/Medigap.

Are Medicare Supplements and Medicare Advantage PPOs the Same?

Dear Toni

What is the difference between a "Medicare Supplement" and a "Medicare Advantage PPO" plan? I am turning 65 and the marketing material, I am being bombarded with absolutely puzzles me.

Friends have informed me that a PPO plan is the same as a supplement because both have a network of doctors to pick from. Look forward to your explanation

Thanks, Joseph from Clear Lake area

Joseph:

You have been given **WRONG i**nformation! With a Medicare Supplement/Medigap, there is not a network of any kind; you have the freedom to use any healthcare provider/facility that will bill Medicare. The Medicare Supplement/Medigap will pay for your Medicare out of pocket expenses that Medicare Parts A and B will not pay.

Medicare Supplements/Medigap and Medicare Advantage Plans are completely different types of Medicare policies.

With a Medicare Advantage PPO, there are lower cost in-network providers/facilities as well as out of network benefits that will cost you more. In 2017, a popular Medicare Advantage PPO plan has a maximum $6,700 in-network out of pocket with a maximum of $9,000 out of network out of pocket.

Most never consider that they could have an out of network provider/facility for their medical claim, but in these current times many healthcare providers/facilities are out of network participants.

If someone decides on a Medicare Advantage PPO plan, remember to verify if your healthcare professional is an in-network or out-of-network provider.

In the Medicare and You Handbook, it explains what a Medicare Supplement/Medigap or a Medicare Advantage PPO plan is.

Below are some of the differences of the two plans:

❖ **Medicare Supplement:**

1) A Medicare Supplement works directly with "Original Medicare". Medicare pays its share of the Medicare-approved amount for "medically necessary "covered healthcare costs
2) Your Medicare Supplement/Medigap will pay its share. With a Medicare Supplement/ Medigap, you chose which doctor, hospital, home health agency, skilled nursing facility, etc. that accepts Medicare assignment for your healthcare. You and your healthcare provider are in control of your healthcare
3) The downside to a Medicare Supplement/Medigap is that you have a monthly premium that may increase each year.
4) Medicare prescription (Part D) drugs plans are not included, so you may want to enroll and will pay separately for a "Stand alone" Medicare (Part D) Prescription drug plan.

❖ **Medicare Advantage PPO Plan:**

1) To qualify for any Medicare Advantage plan:
   a) You must be enrolled in both Medicare Parts A & B.
   b) Live in the service area 6 months out of a year…
   c) Not have end stage renal disease (kidney dialysis)
2) When you choose a Medicare Advantage Plan, then Medicare pays the insurance company a certain amount every month for your care (whether or not you use the benefits) if you are on the plan and your Part B must always be in effect.
3) When you go to the doctor, hospital or visit your pharmacist, you must only use your Medicare Advantage insurance card, not your Medicare (red, white and blue) card.
4) A Medicare Advantage Plan must provide all your Part A and Part B benefits and some Medicare Advantage Plans have Part D prescription drug plans included. Some plans have "extra" benefits such as gym membership, etc.
5) Healthcare facilities, like MD Anderson accept few Medicare Advantage plans. Talk to your provider or facility and make sure they accept the Medicare Advantage plan you want to enroll in whether PPO or HMO. Find out if the Medicare Advantage plans, you are researching are an in network or an out of network provider.

Toni Says® *This is very important)*

Rumor is…Medicare Supplement Plans F & C
Are Going Away After Jan. 1, 2020?

Morning Toni:

I am turning 65 in October and noticing a difference in the premiums between many of the Medicare Supplement plans. F is considerably higher in premium than G and I am wondering why there is such a difference

I have been told from various friends that Plan F is the plan to pick, but I am concerned about there being such a difference in premiums. Many of the plans have a savings of $56 a month or $672 a year when choosing Plan G over Plan F. I don't understand why there is such a difference and would like some clarity on the difference for me not to make a major mistake

Thanks, Sam from Clear Lake, TX

Sam

This week, I received information from one of America's prominent Medicare Supplement insurance companies informing their agents that Medicare Supplement Plans F and C will not be eligible for enrollment after January 1, 2020. Medicare Supplement Plan G will take the place of Medicare Plans F and C

This information confirmed what I had been hearing in the Medicare community that Medicare Plans F and C will no longer be available in 2020.

Congress passed the new legislation called "Medicare Access and CHIP Reauthorization Act of 2015" (MACRA) to help the medical industry by correcting the "Doc Fix" proposal, but the new legislation ended Medicare Supplement's Plans F and C in 2020, which pick up all of Medicare's costs and deductibles

Doctors were concerned about the Medicare cuts to the medical profession and were threatening to leave Medicare

To keep doctors from bailing out of Medicare, Congress had to come up with that money somewhere and they found it in the Part B deductible that Medicare Plans F and C pickup.

Congress decided to pass 200 billion dollars of Medicare expenses over a 10-year period to the Medicare beneficiaries by eliminating Medicare Supplement Plans F and C which pay for Medicare's Part B deductible

The new law of 2015 (MACRA) ensures doctors will be adequately paid for Medicare services and that those enrolled in Medicare have the healthcare professionals they need.

Now, you know why MACRA was passed.

Those who are new to Medicare or wish to apply for a new Medicare Supplement/Medigap need to know that Medicare Plan F and C are available until January 1, 2020. Therefore, you might want to see what Medicare Plan G has to offer

Let's discuss the difference

Plan F: offers more benefits with higher premiums. Those who wish to enroll or currently have Plan F will not be forced to move because this change only affects newly eligible beneficiaries with effective dates of Jan. 1, 2020 and Medicare Plan F will no longer be available.
Plan G offers lower rates with the Medicare Part B deductible not covered and being paid for by the enrolled Medicare beneficiary. In 2021 the Medicare Part B deductible was $203. In 2022 the Medicare Part B deductible was $230. Your out-of-pocket expense would be the Part B deductible for the current year. Medicare Plan G will still be available after Jan. 1, 2020 for all newly enrolled in Medicare Parts A and B

America No Do-Over for Enrolling in Medicare Incorrectly!

Hello, Toni:

My husband retired several years ago when he turned 65. He enrolled in Medicare Part A, but declined Part B because I put him on my Blue Cross Blue Shield policy provided by my employer. Lately I have read articles concerning failure to enroll in Medicare Part B and the additional cost each year that you delay enrollment

I have planned to keep my husband on my policy until my retirement in 3 years when I turn 65. The coverage and cost are better than Part B or any additional supplement on the market. I spoke with a representative at the Social Security office and asked them if he would be penalized for delaying enrollment in Part B. They said he would not as long as he provides evidence that he has maintained health insurance

This information seems counter to what I have been reading or what friends are telling me at church. Help Toni! I am very confused

Shirley from Alvin

Shirley:

Social Security gave you excellent advice about your husband's Medicare. Many times, in the past 5 years, I have written about the famous ***"Special Enrollment Period"*** form that needs to have ***"Special Enrollment Period"*** written at the top in red. You will need to have that form signed by your HR when you leave-your company benefits to avoid the Medicare Part B penalty.

Shirley, you must have this form signed whether you leave for a new job or simply retire. This is necessary!

Last week, I had two different Houston Chronicle readers that came into the Toni Says® office for a Medicare consultation and both had already enrolled in Medicare Parts A and B. Both are now experiencing the pain and agony of trying to enroll in a Medicare Supplement/Medigap as they now must answer health questions.

One was a 67-year-old male employee with company benefits that had enrolled in Medicare Parts A and B in 2015. The other was also a 67-year-old male who was a dependent on his wife's group health benefits, who also had enrolled in Medicare Part B a few years earlier

In both cases they had wives who qualified for the Medicare Supplement Open Enrollment (6-month enrollment period) because their Medicare Parts A and B were beginning April 1 t Neither wife had to answer one health question and picked whichever Medicare Supplement plan they desired. I have written about this special 6-month window, many times and stressed the importance of enrolling in Part B at the correct time.

The two husbands can only apply for a guaranteed issue Medicare Supplement policy because they have been enrolled in Medicare Part B longer than 6 months and have health conditions that keep them from qualifying medically. They can only receive a 63-day guaranteed issue period to apply for a Medicare Supplement, not a 6-month window. You must have a **current** company benefit termination letter to prove to the Medicare Supplement insurance company that you are in a guaranteed issue period.

No termination letter? Then you might not qualify and will only have Original Medicare Parts A and B as your medical plan.

You will only qualify for certain plans during a guaranteed issue period. You will also have the right to buy Medicare Supplement/Medigap Plans A, B, C, F, K or L that's sold in your state by any insurance company. The plans should cover all pre-existing health conditions and cannot charge more premium, regardless of past or present health problems

Medicare Supplement Rate Increase is Killing Me!

Can I Change NOW!!!

Dear Toni

I recently received the renewal for my Medicare Supplement and the rate increase is not in my budget. It is over 15% and every year it seems to go up, but not as much as this year. I'm a 70-year-old female with high blood pressure. I'm confused about changing companies. Heard I have to wait until Medicare open enrollment in October. Can you please tell me what to do?

Signed Cindy a loyal weekly reader

Hello Cindy:

You are not alone. I have heard from many of my readers that their Medicare Supplement insurance companies have had increases. Medicare's Annual Enrollment Period (Open Enrollment) is only for Medicare Advantage plans and/or Medicare Prescription Drug plans and does not include Medicare Supplements/Medigap Policies.

I have talked to more people who want to change their Medicare Supplement/Medigap and do not realize that they can change their Medicare Supplement/Medigap whenever they want. No matter what Medicare Supplement/Medigap you have, it can be changed any day of the year.

The best time to enroll in a Medicare Supplement/Medigap is during your Medigap/Medicare Supplement Open enrollment period. This period is the 6-month period that starts on the first day of the month in which you are 65 years and enrolled in Part B or if you are past 65 and enrolled in Part B for the first time. You do not have to answer any health questions because the Medicare Supplement company you pick must accept you no matter what your health situation is.

From what you have told me, I do not believe this is a guaranteed issue situation and that you will have to answer health questions and meet the insurance companies underwriting requirements. You may want to talk with a few Medicare Supplement companies to see which one you qualify for because of your health conditions and the medications that you are taking. Sometimes changing is not that easy if you cannot meet the underwriting requirements.

Reader Alert You may apply to replace your Medicare Supplement policy at any time. Do not cancel your existing policy until you have been approved by your new insurance company

Need Medicare Supplement Because I've Been Laid Off?

Dear Toni

Last week, I was laid off from my job and now I need to enroll in Medicare Parts A and B. I am 74 years old and am concerned about receiving a Medicare penalty because I never did enroll in Medicare Parts A and B. My wife is 67 and has been enrolled in Medicare, since turning 65

Since turning 65, I have always worked for the same company that now does not supply retiree benefits when no longer working full-time. We can apply for COBRA benefits for 18 months

With my health issues, I believe that we should apply for a Medicare Supplement because of the freedom it provides, from what I have read in the Toni Says® Medicare column

Please explain what I need to do to get a Medicare Supplement for both me and my wife?

Thanks, Bob from Sugar Land, TX

Hello Bob

You need to file the "**Request for Employment Information**" form signed by your company with the local Social Security office to have your Medicare Part B started ASAP and not receive the "famous" Part B penalty because you are past 65.

Don't file this form the correct way and your Part B penalty will go all the way back to the day you turned 65

Since you are receiving Part B for the first time, you will have a one-time special opportunity which is explained in the <u>*Medicare and You Handbook*</u> It *states*

> *"The best time to buy a Medicare Supplement/Medigap policy is during your Medigap Open Enrollment Period. This 6-month period that begins on the first day of the month in which you're 65 or older **and** enrolled in Part B."*

After this enrollment period, you may not be able to buy a Medicare Supplement/Medigap policy, if you're unable to answer health question.

Your wife, Mary must answer questions to apply for a Medicare Supplement/Medigap because she has had Medicare Part B longer than 6 months. If Mary has health issues, then she can qualify as a guarantee issue policy.

Mary's saving grace, if she has a health issue is that you are losing your company benefits and Mary can receive a 63-day guaranteed issue period for applying for a Medicare Supplement/ Medigap plan. Keep your company benefit termination letter to show the Medicare Supplement insurance company that you are in a guarantee issue period.

With guaranteed issue, an insurance company must:

Sell you a Medicare Supplement/Medigap policy. "You have the right to buy Medicare Supplement/ Medigap Plan A, B, C, F, K or L that's sold in your state by any insurance company for those who's Medicare Part A begins prior to January 1, 2020. For those who Medicare Part A with Medicare Part B which begins after January 1, 2020, then Medicare Plan G and High-Deductible Plan G will be offered in place of Medicare Supplement Plan C, Plan F and High-Deductible Plan F.

- Cover all your pre-existing health conditions.
  Cannot charge you more for a Medicare Supplement/Medigap policy, regardless of past or present health problems.

Bottom line enrolling in Part B the correct way is so important, while "still working" full-time with true company benefits whether you are the working or non-working spouse. Not only to keep from receiving a Medicare Part B penalty, but also to be able to enroll and be accepted in any Medicare Supplement/Medigap plan.

Toni Says® America needs to realize the value of Medicare Part B

Oil Companies Dropping Retiree Medicare Plans!!

Know Your Medicare Options?

Help Toni:

I am so nervous over what is happening with my husband's retirement benefits. He worked for Chevron for over 30 years and beginning January 1st we will not have any company benefits

What do I do NOW? I am a 73-year-old female who has never purchased insurance before and have no idea of what to look for. My husband, Paul who is 77 is in the end stages of Alzheimer's and cannot help me with this transition

You understand Medicare and can explain to me what I need to do in such easy terms that I can comprehend. I cannot afford to make a costly mistake because the Alzheimer's facility is costing over $7,000 a month for Paul's care

~ ***Thanks in advance…Charlotte from Spring Branch area***

Hello Ms. Charlotte

You are about the 4th person this week which contacted me about losing retiree benefits because their company is either not covering the retirees and spouses or moving retirees to a Medicare Advantage plan that will save the company's bottom line.

This trend of companies not covering retirees began during 2013's Medicare Open Enrollment Period with Baker Hughes, TRS and CITGO to name a few companies not covering their retirees. The next year, Schlumberger and Marathon Oil changed their retirement options.

From the information that I have read, if you do not make the change, then you will lose any help from your retirement company with the HRA (health reimbursement account) benefits checks coming from whom you retired from.

I am sure that there are others having the same problem because the letters informing the retirees are beginning to arrive in their mailbox.

Don't **WORRY!!** There is light at the end of the tunnel!! You have two options to pick from that the Medicare programs which your retiree benefits Medicare Plans offer:

Option #1: Medicare Supplement with a Medicare Prescription Drug Plan (Part D)

Works directly with "Original Medicare" and gives more freedom to go to any healthcare facility, provider or doctor who accepts Medicare assignment. Charlotte, you have retirement benefits and since your retirement company, has sent you and your husband, Paul, a letter saying that you will have no medical insurance coverage after December 31 ^{t}, both you and your husband will have guaranteed issue *(which means you do not have to answer health questions and your Medicare Supplement insurance policy will be issued)* Guaranteed issue is for certain Medicare Supplement/Medigap plans depending on the insurance company you apply with. You will have 63 days to apply and receive guaranteed issue for a Medicare Supplement because you are currently "not working" and retired on company benefits. You will want to search for a Medicare Part D plan that fits your needs and covers all your drugs. Call Medicare at 1/800-MEDICARE (633-4227) *or go online at* **www.medicare.gov** to see which Part D Plan fits your needs. You will have the same 63 days to enroll in a Medicare Part D plan without receiving a Part D (LEP) penalty.

Option #2: Medicare Advantage Plan with or without Part D

Talk with your doctor about changing from "Original Medicare" to a Medicare Advantage plan. Make sure your doctor or healthcare facility accepts the Medicare Advantage plan that you are exploring. Many Medicare Advantage plans contain Medicare Part D, then you may not have to enroll in a separate Part D plan.

If you have any other questions concerning losing your retirement benefits or searching for the right Medicare plan, email the Toni Says® office at **info@tonisays.com** and our staff will assist you.

Which Medicare Plan Travels with Me While I Travel the US?

Toni

I have retired effective January 1 and now my wife and I are going to travel the US in the new Winnebago that is sitting in my driveway. I am having a hard time trying to sign up for Medicare since I turn 65 in February and really do not know what my address will be since I will be traveling at different times of the year

I am an insulin dependent diabetic and will need easy access to a pharmacy while traveling, plus if I have an emergency I do want access to decent medical care anywhere in the US

Please give me your thoughts on my situation and what would be the best option for me and my wife

Thanks, Joseph from Cypress, TX

Well, Joseph:

Planning your Medicare is an important part of planning your retirement because one wrong move can cause you thousands of your hard-earned retirement dollars.

Many new to Medicare miss a special window of opportunity when they first enroll in Medicare Part B. This special time is called the Medicare Supplement/Medigap Open Enrollment period and lastsfor 6 months beginning the first day of the month in which you are 65 or older and enrolled in Part B.

During this special period, an insurance company cannot use medical underwriting because of any health problems.

Joseph, if you enroll in the special 6-month window, being an insulin dependent diabetic, will not affect you enrolling in a Medicare Supplement/Medigap Policy.

Touring the US may be another reason to choose a Medicare Supplement/Medigap Policy because there is not a network and if the healthcare provider or facility is accepting Medicare, then you can receive your care there.

Also, you will want to take time when picking your Medicare Part D plan because you will want access to a nationwide pharmacy that is not only in your Cypress, TX area, but also in other parts of the country.

Another option for both healthcare and prescript drugs is a Medicare Advantage (Part C) plan which may or may not offer the flexibility of easy access to healthcare providers in various areas of the country.

Below are some of the differences between a Medicare Supplement/Medigap and a Medicare Advantage Plan

❖ **Medicare Supplement/Medigap:**

1. A Medicare Supplement/Medigap works directly with "Original/Traditional Medicare"
2. You chose which doctor, hospital, home health agency, skilled nursing facility, etc. that accepts Medicare assignment for your healthcare.
3. There is a monthly premium that may increase each year.
4. You may enroll and will pay separately for a "Stand alone" Medicare (Part D) Prescription drug plan.

❖ **Medicare Advantage Plan:**

1. To qualify for the plan:
    a) You must be enrolled in both Medicare Parts A & B.
    b) Live in the service area 6 months out of a year or change when you are out of the area.
    c) Not have end stage renal disease (kidney dialysis).
2. Check with your doctors/hospitals to be sure they are in the plan's network before you enroll.
3. You must use your Medicare Advantage insurance card, not your Medicare (red, white, and blue) card
4. A Medicare Advantage Plan must provide all your Part A and Part B benefits and some Medicare Advantage Plans have Part D prescription drug plans included.
5. A Medicare Advantage Plan may have a zero to low dollar premiums
6. With a Medicare Advantage plan, you may have different co pays, co-insurances or deductibles to pay and have maximum out of pocket expenses to meet.

Chapter 4
Medicare Part C
Or
Medicare Advantage Plan

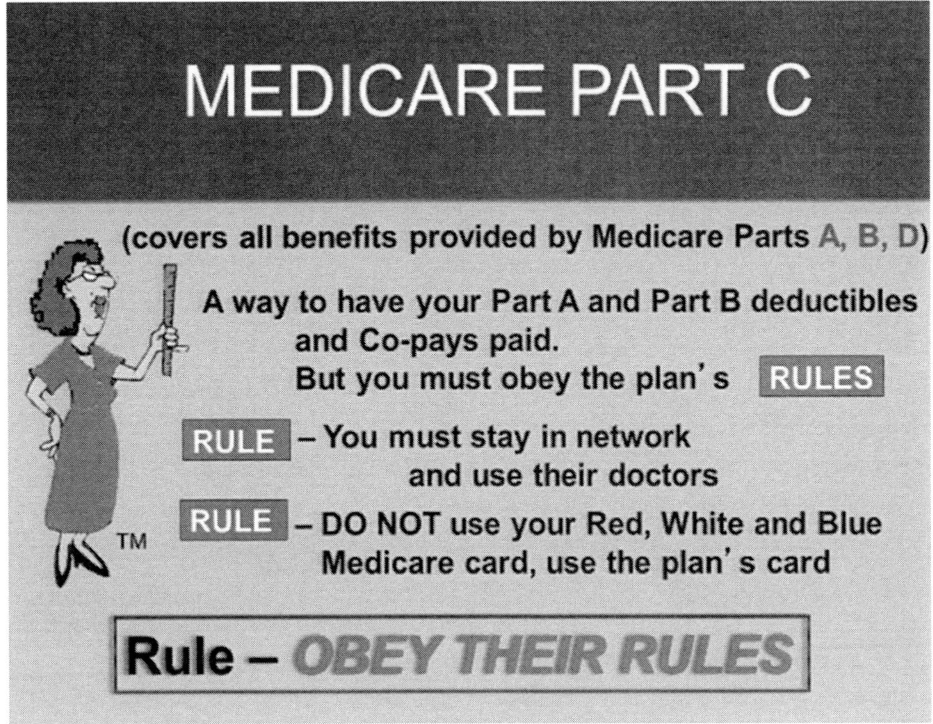

MEDICARE PART C (Medicare Advantage Plan)

Part C is another way to get your Medicare benefits and also have what Original/Traditional Medicare does not pay for paid by the Medicare Advantage Plan. There can be co pays to pay, but Part C can help with your out of pocket expenses. Private insurance companies approved by Medicare manage Part C. These Medicare Advantage plans must cover medically necessary services, but can charge different co-payments, co-insurance, or deductibles for these services.

What are Medicare Advantage Plans?

Medicare Advantage Plan or Part C is a health plan option (HMO, PPO, PFFS, MSA & SNP) approved by Medicare, which are run by private insurance companies. These plans are part of the Medicare program. You do not lose your Medicare; you just don't use your Medicare card! Remember, you must take only your Medicare Advantage Insurance Card to your doctor and use only the new Medicare Advantage Card from the company that you enrolled with.

Medicare pays the private health insurance company a set amount each month for as long as you stay on their plan. The private insurance company pays for all of your health care. The insurance companies and agents must follow strict rules set by Medicare. A Medicare Advantage Plan is **NOT** a supplemental insurance policy.

If you are on a fixed budget or have a health problem that prevents you from changing your Medicare supplement/Medigap due to the rising costs, there is hope for you or as they say, "Light at the end of the Tunnel". A Medicare Advantage Plan may be just for you!!

A Medicare Advantage Plan does not scrimp on your care and it DOES take care of your health care needs. Medicare health Insurance plans with doctor, hospital and prescription drugs are called Medicare Advantage Prescription Drugs or MAPD. Also, Medicare health insurance plans with just hospital and doctor care and no prescription drug coverage are Medicare Advantage or MA plans. Both Part C "Medicare Advantage plans" whether MAPD or MA provide all of your Part A *(hospital insurance)* and Part B *(Medicare Insurance)* benefits. They must cover all medically necessary services that Original/ Traditional Medicare Plan provides. Medicare Advantage Plans can charge copayments, coinsurance, and deductibles for all services

Medicare Advantage Plans offer extra benefits that Original Medicare does not offer, such as vision, hearing, dental, diet, and exercise programs. Most Medicare Advantage Plans have a network of providers. You may need referrals to see a specialist. Remember when you use providers/specialists that are out of network, you may pay an out of network fee, a higher co pay or you may pay ALL of the cost, depending on the plan you choose. It is less expensive to stay in network. Check the network to make sure you like the doctors and hospitals before you join any Medicare Advantage Plans

Toni Says® Call any Medicare Advantage plan before joining to find out what the services cost and make sure that the Medicare Advantage plan meets your needs. Check the Medicare Advantage plan that you want to change to especially the network of hospitals, doctors and other providers. Always know what you are jumping into. The agent that is enrolling you in the plan sometimes does not know all the down falls a plan could have.

Reader Alert CHECK YOUR HOSPITAL AND DOCTOR BEFORE YOU ATTEMPT TO ENROLL IN A PART C MEDICARE ADVANTAGE PLAN. FIND OUT IF THEY ACCEPT THE PLAN YOU ARE CHOSING

Different Types of Medicare Advantage Plans

Different parts of the country have different types of Medicare Advantage Plans, and are based mainly on how many Medicare beneficiaries are in that area. If your area is a rural area, you won't have the same plans as your sister in a big city, because there are not as many people on Medicare in your area. That is really sad, because the ones who need the better plans the most, seem to be left out. The following are 5 Medicare Advantage Plans that are used the most throughout the country. I will go through them with you and give you some idea of what they are like.

1) **Health Maintenance Organization (HMO):** *Available in limited areas of the country* with an HMO; you have certain doctors, specialists, or hospitals to which you MUST go, except in an emergency. Your out of pocket cost will be lower than Original/Traditional Medicare, BUT you must stay in network or you WILL PAY 100% out of pocket, except if it is a life-threatening emergency. That means you have no choice of where you are taken due to a stroke, a heart attack,

accident, or if you are out of town on vacation, other life-threatening events, etc. *(Please see chart on Medicare Advantage Plans*

2) **<u>Private Provider Organization (PPO):</u>** *Available in local or regional* You will have less out of pocket when you use network providers, <u>BUT</u> you <u>CAN</u> go out of network and you will pay higher costs. Most PPO networks are nationwide. These plans differ from an HMO because you may have slightly more out of pocket costs and the premiums may be more than the HMO. You will have more flexibility and more control in your hands about your health care. *(Please see chart on Medicare Advantage Plans)*
3) **<u>Private Fee For Service (PFFS)</u>** *Available all over the country* This is the newest of all Medicare Advantage plans. You may go to any Medicare approved doctor or hospital that accepts the plans payment, but the doctor must agree to bill the insurance company. The insurance company, rather than Medicare, decides how much to pay providers and how much you will pay for services. You may pay more or less for services than on Original Medicare and you may have extra benefits that Original/Traditional Medicare does not cover. *(Please see chart on Medicare Advantage Plans)*
4) **<u>Medical Savings Account (MSA):</u>** *Available all over the country* combines a high deductible Medicare Advantage Plan and a bank account. The plan deposits money from Medicare directly into the bank account, which is used to pay medical expenses until your Medicare deductible is met. Not very many companies market this plan. Be very careful when looking at this option because this plan has uncharted waters. Not very many people with Medicare are on these plans. *(Please see chart on Medicare Advantage Plans)*
5) **<u>Special Needs Plan (SNP)</u>** *Available in certain areas of the country.* This is a special type of MA plan which provides more specialized health care for specific groups, such as those on Medicare and Medicaid and those with chronic medical problems, such as diabetes, COPD, congestive heart failure, arthritis, etc. These plans give extra benefits, such as disease specific prescription drugs, which are carried through the "donut hole". *(Please see the following chart on Medicare Advantage Plans.)*

Chart of Medicare Advantage Plans

Medicare Advantage Plan Choices					
	HMO (Health Maintenance Organization)	**PPO** (Preferred Provider Organization)	**PFFS** (Private Fee for Service)	**MSA** (Medical Savings Account)	**SNP** (Special Needs Plan)
Are prescription drugs covered?	Yes	Yes, but check to be sure	Sometimes	No	Yes
Do I need to choose a primary care doctor?	Yes, Must be in the plan.	No, in or out of network	No	No	Depends on the plan
Can I choose any doctor or hospital?	No, must be in the plan	Yes, in or out of network	Yes, but not if your plan has a network	Yes	Must be in the plan
Can I choose to go to a specialist?	No, you must get a referral	Yes, in or out of network	Yes, but not if your plan has a network	Yes	Must be in the plan
Other useful information about the plan.	Know and follow the rules carefully	Some plans offer additional benefits for an additional premium.	This is not the same as original Medicare. These are private insurance companies. Make sure your Doctor, and Hospital are willing to accept the plan's payment terms. Plan may have a network	These are 2-part plans: a high deductible health plan and a bank account. *You can use the money in your bank account to pay for your health	These are for people with chronic disabling conditions, living in a nursing home (require nursing care at home or eligible for Medicare and Medicaid *The plan manages your health care needs

Rules for Enrolling in a Medicare Advantage Plan

1) You must have both Part A and Part B. Do not ever cancel your Part B or you lose your Medicare Advantage Plan. Be sure to continue to pay the Part B premium or you will lose Part B.
2) You must live in a certain area and if you move out of the area, you may enroll in a new Medicare Advantage Plan in your new area.
3) You must not have End-Stage Renal Disease (permanent kidney failure).
4) Enrollment dates apply so REMEMBER TO CHECK YOUR ENROLLMENT DATES! Please review enrollment periods below.

Initial Coverage Election Period

Turning 65 or the 1 t time on Medicare (Disability for under 65 years)

- ***3 months before the effective date Part B,***
- ***effective date of part B,***
- ***3 months after the effective date Part B***

You should enroll in one of these to have prescription drug coverage during your Initial Coverage Election enrollment period:

1) **MAPD** ***(Medicare Advantage Plan)***
2) **PDP** ***(Prescription Drug Plan)***

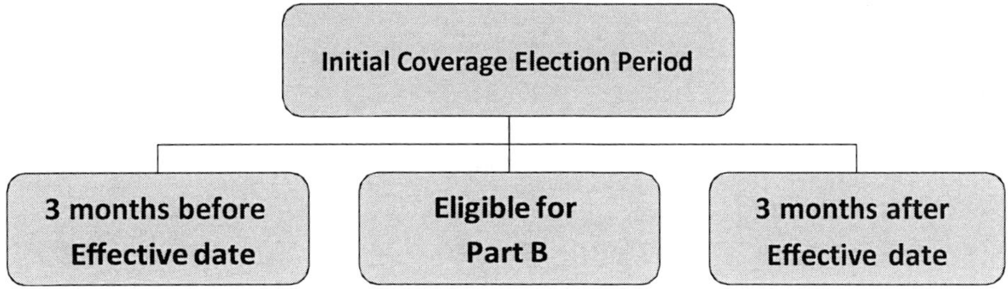

Know Your Enrollment Dates

October 15–December 7th (each year) – Annual Election Period

Consumers can make a new plan choice. During the Annual Election Period (AEP), any Medicare Beneficiary may elect to join a Part C Medicare Advantage Plan or Part D Medicare Prescription Drug Plan for the first time, or switch to a different plan. Any elections made during the AEP become effective January 1. During this time, you are able to:

Purchase a Part D Medicare Prescription Drug Plan.
Change from one Medicare Prescription Drug Plan to a new Medicare Prescription Drug Plan
Enroll in a Medicare Advantage Plan with Prescription Drugs.
Change from one Medicare Advantage Plan to a new Medicare Advantage Plan.
Return to Original/Traditional Medicare and purchase a Medicare Supplement/ Medigap and enroll in a Part D Medicare Prescription Drug Plan.
Return to Original Medicare and enroll in a Part D Medicare Prescription Drug Plan.

January 1 - March 31 (each year) - Medicare Advantage Open Enrollment Period

During the Medicare Advantage Open Enrollment Period (MA OEP), you can switch from your Medicare Advantage Plan to another MA Plan, or to Original Medicare with or without a Part D plan, The MA OEP occurs each year from January 1 through March 31. You can only use this period if you have a Medicare Advantage Plan.

April 1 – December 31 - Lock In

On April 1, you will be locked into whatever plan you have chosen and will not be able to change until the Annual Enrollment Period (AEP) for the next year. In other words, consumers must remain with their last choice through the end of the year unless they qualify for a SEP.

Reader Alert It is important that you have explored all of your options, and are satisfied with your choice

***Special Enrollment Period* (SEP) for Medicare Advantage Plans**- see the Medicare and You Handbook

What are *Special Enrollment Periods* (SEP) for Medicare Advantage Plans?

In most cases, you must stay enrolled for that calendar year starting the date your coverage begins. However, in certain situations, you may be able to join, switch, or drop a Medicare Advantage plan at other times

Some of these situations include the following:

- Loss of Creditable Coverage (insurance through an employer)
- Move into or out of a plan service area
- Eligible for Medicaid (dual eligibility)
- Qualify for or have a change to your Low-Income Status (LIS)
- You live in a long-term care facility
- Qualify for a Special Needs Plan (SNP)

If You Enroll in a Medicare Advantage Plan

- You are still in the Medicare program.
- You still have Medicare rights and protections including the right to appeal.
- You can enroll or switch plans only during certain times of the year.
- You may have a monthly premium.
- You may have to use plan providers

***Note** ****IMPORTANT TO STAY IN NETWORK**

- You don't need to purchase a Medicare Supplement/Medigap Policy. The Medicare Supplement/ Medigap cannot pay the Medicare Advantage Plan deductibles, co-pays or co-insurances. An insurance agent cannot enroll you in a Medicare Advantage plan if you are enrolled in a Medicare Supplement/Medigap Policy.
- If you see a doctor who is not in the plan, your services may not be covered or your costs may be higher. Check and see if your plan has out of network benefits
- Plan benefits may change each year. The plan will send you changes each fall for the next year.

- If your plan decides to no longer participate in the Medicare program, you will have to enroll in another Medicare Advantage Plan or go back to Original/Traditional Medicareand get a Stand-Alone Medicare Prescription Drug Plan to go with it. You might choose a Medicare Supplement/Medigap and enroll in a Stand-Alone Medicare Prescription Drug Plan. Remember, that the Medicare Enrollment rules will apply.

Search through the table of contents for your specific Medicare Part C (Medicare Advantage Plan) questions or read the rest of this chapter and gain Medicare Part C (Medicare Advantage Plan) knowledge to help yourself or your friends that are confused. Below are articles from the Toni Says® newspaper column regarding specific questions about Medicare Part C (Medicare Advantage Plan).

Are Medicare Supplements/Medigap and Medicare Advantage PPOs the Same?

Dear Toni

What is the difference between a "Medicare Supplement" and a "Medicare Advantage PPO" plan? I am turning 65 and the marketing material I am being bombarded with absolutely puzzles me.

Friends have informed me that a PPO plan is the same as a supplement because both have a network of doctors to pick from. Look forward to your explanation

Thanks, Joseph from Clear Lake area

Joseph:

You have been given **WRONG i**nformation! With a Medicare Supplement/Medigap, there is not a network of any kind; you have the freedom to use any healthcare provider/facility that will bill Medicare. The Medicare Supplement/Medigap will pay for your Medicare out of pocket that Medicare Parts A and B will not pay.

Medicare Supplements/Medigap and Medicare Advantage Plans are completely different types of Medicare policies.

With a Medicare Advantage PPO, there are lower cost in-network providers/facilities as well as out of network benefits that will cost you more. Out of pocket maximum can change each year. On average, a Medicare Advantage PPO plan has a maximum $6,700 in-network out of pocket with a maximum of $9,000 out of network out of pocket.

Those enrolled in a Medicare Advantage PPO plan, never consider that they could have an out of network provider/facility for their medical claim, but in these current times many healthcare providers/facilities are out of network participants.

If you decide on a Medicare Advantage PPO plan, remember to verify if your healthcare professional is an in-network or out-of-network provider.

In the Medicare and You Handbook, it explains what a Medicare Supplement or a Medicare Advantage PPO plan is.

Below are some of the differences of the two plans:

❖ **Medicare Supplement:**

5) A Medicare Supplement works directly with "Original Medicare". Medicare pays its share of the Medicare-approved amount for "medically necessary "covered healthcare costs
6) Your Medicare Supplement/Medigap will pay its share. With a Medicare Supplement/ Medigap, you chose which doctor, hospital, home health agency, skilled nursing facility, etc. that accepts Medicare assignment for your healthcare. You and your healthcare provider are in control of your healthcare
7) The downside to a Medicare Supplement/Medigap is that you have a monthly premium that may increase the premium rate each year.
8) Medicare prescription (Part D) drugs plans are not included, so you may want to enroll and will pay separately for a "Stand alone" Medicare (Part D) Prescription drug plan.

❖ **Medicare Advantage PPO Plan:**

6) To qualify for any Medicare Advantage plan:
    a. You must be enrolled in both Medicare Parts A & B
    b. Live in the service area 6 months out of a year
    c. Not have end stage renal disease (kidney dialysis)
7) When you choose a Medicare Advantage Plan, then Medicare pays the insurance company a certain amount every month for your care if you are on the plan. Your Part B must always be in effect
8) When you go to the doctor, hospital or visit your pharmacist, you must only use your Medicare Advantage insurance card, not your Medicare (red, white and blue) card.
9) A Medicare Advantage Plan must provide all your Part A and Part B benefits and some Medicare Advantage Plans have Part D prescription drug plans included. The Plan can also have "extra" benefits such as gym membership, etc.
10) Healthcare facilities, like MD Anderson accept few Medicare Advantage plans. Talk to your provider or facility and make sure they accept the Medicare Advantage plan you want to enroll in whether PPO or HMO. Find out if the Medicare Advantage plans, you are researching are an in network or an out of network provider. *(This is very important)*

Get Me Out of this Medicare Advantage Mistake!!

Toni

Last year, I made a big mistake and changed to a Medicare Advantage HMO from my Medicare Supplement and I want out!! ...I cannot even get a MRI with this company, because most of the doctors are not accepting this plan. What can I do?

Signed...George in Mobile, AL

Dear George:

You can go back to "Original/Traditional Medicare' and enroll-in a new Medicare Supplement/ Medigap during Medicare's Open Enrollment starting October 15, and it will end at midnight on December 7th (Pearl Harbor Day).

For you to disenroll from your Medicare Advantage company, what you need to do is enroll with a Medicare Prescription Drug plan. You will automatically be out of your old Advantage plan and back to "Original/Traditional Medicare" with a Medicare Prescription Drug plan; then apply for a Medicare Supplement/Medigap to pick up what Medicare does not pay for.

An important Medicare rule is that if this is your **first year** out of a Medicare Supplement/ Medigap, you may have **guaranteed issue** (which means you can return to the Medicare Supplement company and plan that you previously had and not have to answer health questions) so if you have a serious illness such as cancer, diabetes, COPD etc. then you can get the same coverage

If you have been with a Medicare Advantage plan longer than a year, then you do not have guaranteed issue, when you decide to return back to "Original/Traditional Medicare", you will have to answer the insurance company's health questions.

Open Enrollment Period or OEP is also the time when you can make changes to your Part D plan or Medicare Advantage plan or you can enroll In a Medicare Part D plan if you missed your enrollment time when you were first eligible.

What can you do during Medicare Open Enrollment:

- Enroll in a new Part D Medicare Prescription Drug Plan which automatically disenrolls you from a Medicare Advantage plan.
  Enroll in a new Part D Medicare Prescription Drug Plan when you have never been in Part D from the time you have been with Medicare.
- Change from one Part D Medicare Prescription Drug Plan to a new Part D Medicare Prescription Drug Plan.
- Enroll in a Part C Medicare Advantage Plan with Prescription Drugs
- Change from one Part C Medicare Advantage Plan to a new Part C Medicare Advantage Plan
- Return to Original Medicare and purchase a Medicare Supplement/Medigap and enroll in a Part D Medicare Prescription Drug Plan.
  Return to Original/Traditional Medicare only and enroll in a Part D Medicare Prescription Drug Plan
- Or Return to Original/Traditional Medicare with no Part D plan.

Reader Alert *Don't forget there is a penalty for not enrolling in a Part D Medicare Prescription Drug plan when you are first eligible*

Need Help Picking Right Medicare Advantage Plan for Mom!!

Dear Toni

My mother is retiring and losing her company benefits. I need help finding a Medicare Advantage plan that can better meet her medical needs

She receives $1,134 on her Social Security check and cannot afford to purchase a Medicare supplement. Can you give me some direction on what I can do to help my mother make a better choice in picking a Medicare Advantage plan? I look forward to what advice you have since you counsel people on Medicare every day

Thank you, Becky from Memphis, TN

Hello Becky:

I know how confusing enrolling in the right Medicare Advantage plan is for your mother because I talk to clients every day who ask the same question. I also help my own mother!!

Here is step by step what you can do to help your mother make the best pick for her Medicare Advantage plans or Medicare health plans as it is called in the Medicare and You Handbook

1) Talk to her primary care physician or specialists to see which Medicare Advantage plans, they are still accepting.
2) Go to **www.Medicare.gov** which has the best tool for helping you narrow your search for Medicare Advantage or Medicare health or drug plan.
    - Click on "Compare Drug and Health Plans" and enter your zip code. You can use the plan finder to compare the different Medicare Advantage plans or even compare standalone (Part D) Medicare Prescription Drug plans.
      The Medicare Plan Finder can compare three (3) plans at a time. You can compare HMOs, PPOs, and PFFS plans.

    ✍ ***Note**: Medicare plan finder only compares Medicare Advantage plans not Medicare Supplements/Medigap.

3) With Medicare HMOs, there is less out of pocket, but you may have more restrictions because some Medicare HMOs must have "Referrals" and some HMOs have "Open Access" options which says that you can go to any specialist without referrals as long as they are in the provider directory, but you may have more out of pocket with an Open Access option.
4) Medicare PPOs and PFFS plans may have fewer restrictions, but may have more out of pocket for the freedom of picking in network or out of network providers. You will pay more for out of network providers.
5) Areas in the summary of benefits for Medicare Advantage plan you need to review:

    Maximum out of pocket-This is the most she will have to pay in a year. Many are not aware that Medicare Advantage plans have maximum out of pocket.

    b. Doctor/specialist co-pays

    c. Inpatient hospital care-
    - Some plans have a single co-pay such as $300 or $500 per stay *(example only)*
    - Some plans are $175 co-pay per day for 20 days which can be a maximum $3500 if you are in the hospital for over 20 days or might be $150 co-pay per day for days 1-5 with a maximum of $750 maximum stay if you are inpatient hospital for more than 5 days *(examples only)*

    d. Outpatient services/surgery
    - Some plans have 1 co-pay for $100 per stay *(example only)*
    - Some plans have 20% or 30% outpatient charge. *(example only)*

    e. Ask what the co-pay is for Chemotherapy or radiation. This may meet maximum out of pocket.

    f. Prescription drug has a formulary with co-pays so make sure her prescriptions are covered.

    g. Skilled nursing out of pocket-this varies with each Medicare Advantage plan.

Now You Don't Like Your Medicare Advantage Plan?

Hello Toni:

My question is, if I change to an Advantage plan and find out in a few months it's not working for me; what are my chances of returning to regular Medicare and a supplement

I have a supplement that is $260 monthly. I am looking for something more reasonable. My age is 73 and in fairly good health. I just found out my regular doctor does not take this plan or I would have to change doctors

I'm mainly concerned that hospitals will not accept the Advantage plan? I've been hearing a lot about doctors and now hospitals not accepting insurance plans because of Obamacare. I have spent hours on the medicare.gov site, but cannot find out what doctors and hospitals are in the networks. I am just as confused as I can be

Thanks, Nancy, Tampa, Florida

Hi there, Nancy:

Medicare's open enrollment ends each year on December 7th at mid-night and those who have made changes to their Medicare options or enroll in a Part C Medicare Advantage plan should receive their new insurance card by January 1 t

Good News…For those who are not happy with the Medicare Advantage plan that they have picked for 2020, on page 72 of the Toni Says® Medicare Survival Guide® Advanced edition, it explains how you can disenroll from the Medicare Advantage Plan. This time is called the **Medicare Advantage Open Enrollment Period** and begin January 1-March 31(each year).

During the Medicare Advantage Open Enrollment Period (MA OEP), you can switch from your Medicare Advantage Plan to another MA Plan, or to Original Medicare with or without a Part D plan. You can only use this period if you have a Medicare Advantage Plan not to change a stand-alone Medicare Part D plan.

You would think that Medicare would give you time to tryout a new Medicare Advantage plan and change to another option…but Medicare doesn't!!

To disenroll from a Medicare Advantage plan after March 31 t, you cannot because you are in "**lock in**" from April 1 t to December 3 t You will now have to wait until the next Medicare enrollment period, which begins October 15 thru December 7th to make your change for the next year with a start date of January 1 t

Nancy, you asked about your hospital accepting Medicare Advantage plans. Most of the hospitals are part of many of the Medicare Advantage networks. Primary care physicians or specialist are a different story because they accept Medicare Advantage plans differently. I always advise my clients and those who attend my "Confused about Medicare" workshops to call all of their doctors to see what plans the healthcare professional/facility accepts.

One thing to remember is that the doctor can also stop taking a plan in the middle of the year. If you find a Medicare Advantage plan that you like and your doctor is not in the plan, then you might have to change doctors to use that plan.

Since you are spending about $260 on a Medicare Supplement/Medigap and want something less expensive with the same access to doctors that accept "Original/Traditional Medicare". An option you might consider would be to shop for a different, less expensive Medicare Supplement/ Medigap such as plan G or Plan N.

Toni Says® The most important thing to remember is to always talk to your doctor or the doctor's office manager before you make any changes to your Medicare insurance needs and see what Medicare Advantage plan they accept.

Dad's Medicare Advantage HMO

Not Accepted by MD Anderson…What Can He Do?

Good Morning Ms. Toni:

I did not realize I could have chosen a Medicare Supplement instead of a Medicare Advantage plan when my Medicare Part B began this February after losing my job with company benefits. I understand from your article, I have a 6-month Medicare Medigap/Supplement open enrollment issue period because I am now enrolled in Part B

I need help disenrolling from this Medicare Advantage plan and go back to Traditional Medicare with a Medicare supplement. Time is ticking and I need to do this fast!! I have recently moved to Houston from Little Rock

Thanks, James

Hi there, James and Welcome to Texas:

Thank you for the great compliment!! I know how overwhelming it can be to understand the rules of Medicare, especially when you are stressed due to an illness.

Below is how I help clients who contact me and want to disenroll from their Medicare Advantage plan and return to Traditional also known as Original Medicare.

There is a "***Special Enrollment Period*** or SEP" to help you qualify for a change of your Medicare Advantage plan. A ***Special Enrollment Period*** or SEP is a certain situation when you are able to join, switch or drop a Medicare Advantage Plan. The special situation

- Moving Out of Area: Is when you have moved out of your area such as when James moved from Arkansas to the Houston area
- Enrolled in Medicaid
- Qualify for Extra Help for prescription drugs.
- Moving into a long-term care facility such as:
    - Skilled nursing facility.
    - Assisted living facility,
    - Personal care home
    - Alzheimer's assisted living facilities.
- Loss of creditable prescription drug coverage. (insurance through your employer).

The trick to disenrolling from a Medicare Advantage Plan, when a SEP is granted, is to enroll in a Stand-alone Part D plan which will automatically disenroll-you from your Advantage plan and back to Original/Traditional Medicare. This will be effective on the 1 t of the next month

Receiving Medicare Supplement Open Enrollment: James because you enrolled in Part B this February, you are within your 6-month Medicare open enrollment period which ends on July 30th you can therefore receive guaranteed issue. Medicare's definition for guaranteed issue is that your acceptance in any Medicare Supplement plan is guaranteed during your Medicare supplement open enrollment period which lasts for 6 months, beginning the first day of the month in which you are either age 65 or older and have just enrolled in Medicare Part B.

If you wait past 6 months from enrolling in Part B then you must qualify with Medical underwriting. James. you received a "little blessing" when you read my article and learned you have other Medicare options to choose from.

Oil Companies Dropping Retiree Medicare Plans!!

Know Your Medicare Options?

Help Toni:

I am so nervous over what is happening with my husband's retirement benefits. He worked for Chevron for over 30 years and beginning January 1st we will not have any company benefits

What do I do NOW? I am a 73-year-old female who has never purchased insurance before and have no idea of what to look for. My husband, Paul who is 77 is in the end stages of Alzheimer's and cannot help me with this transition

You understand Medicare and can explain to me what I need to do in such easy terms that I can comprehend. I cannot afford to make a costly mistake because the Alzheimer's facility is costing over $7,000 a month for Paul's care

Thanks in advance...Charlotte from Spring Branch area

Hello Ms. Charlotte

You are about the 4th person this week who contacted me about losing retiree benefits because their company is either not covering the retirees and spouses or moving retirees to a Medicare Advantage plan that will save the company's bottom line.

This trend of companies not covering retirees began during 2013's Medicare Open Enrollment Period with Baker Hughes, TRS and CITGO to name a few companies not covering their retirees. The next year, Schlumberger and Marathon Oil changed their retirement options.

From the information that I have read, if you do not make the change, then you will lose any help from your retirement company with the HRA (health reimbursement account) benefits checks coming from who you retired from.

I am sure that there are others having the same problem because letters informing the retirees continue to arrive in the mailbox each year.

Don't **WORRY!!** There is light at the end of the tunnel!! You have two options to pick from the Medicare programs which your retiree benefits Medicare plans of er

Option #1: <u>Medicare Supplement with a Medicare Prescription Drug Plan (Part D)</u>

Works directly with "Original/Traditional Medicare" and gives more freedom to go to any healthcare facility, provider or doctor who accepts Medicare assignment. Charlotte, you have retirement benefits and since your retirement company, has sent you and your husband, Paul, a letter saying that you will have no medical insurance coverage after December 3 t, both you and your husband will have guaranteed issue *(which means you do not have to answer health questions and your Medicare Supplement insurance policy will be issued)* Guaranteed issue is for certain Medicare Supplement plans depending on the insurance company you apply. You will have 63 days to apply and receive guaranteed issue for a Medicare Supplement because you are currently "not working" and retired on company benefits You will want to searchfor a Medicare Part D plan that fits your needs and covers all your drugs. Call Medicare at 1/800-MEDICARE (633-4227) *or go online at* **www.medicare.gov** to see which Part D Plan fits your needs. You will have the same 63 days to enroll in a Medicare Part D plan without receiving a Part D (LEP) penalty.

Option #2: Medicare Advantage Plan with or without Part D

Talk with your doctor about changing from "Original/Traditional Medicare" to a Medicare Advantage plan. Make sure your doctor or healthcare facility accepts the Medicare Advantage plan that you are exploring. Many Medicare Advantage plans contain Medicare Part D, then you may not have to enroll in a separate Part D plan.

If you have any other questions concerning losing your retirement benefits or searching for the right Medicare plan, email the Toni Says® office at **info@tonisays.com.**

Turning 65 with Cancer…Is Medicare Advantage Right for Me?

Hi Toni

I am turning 65 this August and have no idea what I should do because I have lung cancer. Currently I am on a COBRA policy from my old employer with all of my medical bills now being paid because I have met my deductible

I receive all of my care from MD Anderson and am taking chemotherapy with my radiation treatments to start in July

Do I enroll in Original Medicare with a Medicare supplement and get Part D, go with a Medicare Advantage plan or stay with my current COBRA plan until it ends in about 15 months? If you could help me sort this out I would greatly appreciate your help

Jonathon from Sugar Land, TX

Hello Jon

Recently, I had a phone call from a frantic daughter, who was trying to help her father who had been diagnosed with pancreatic cancer and he had chosen a Medicare Advantage HMO when he turned 65. Now her father has to wait until Medicare's annual enrollment in the fall to make a change back to Original/Traditional Medicare because MD Anderson is not in that Medicare Advantage plan's HMO network

February 15th of every year begins lock-in for Medicare Advantage plans which means everyone enrolled in a Medicare Advantage Plan will have to wait until October 15th –December 7th to make any changes back to Original/Traditional Medicare for the following year

I have good news for you, Jon, because you are turning 65 in August, there is a **special enrollment time** called Medicare Supplement/Medigap open enrollment.

As I have said before, this is the best time for someone to purchase a Medicare Supplement/ Medigap because the open enrollment lasts for a 6-month period beginning the first day of the month in which you are 65 or older and have just enrolled in Part B for the first time

During this open enrollment period, you may enroll in a Medicare Supplement/Medigap Plan and not have to answer any health questions to be accepted by any Medicare Supplement Plan.

If you decide not to keep your COBRA plan, you do not have to worry about your medical care being taking care of with the Medicare Supplement/Medigap, but after the 6-month window, you will have to submit to a complete underwritten application for a Medicare Supplement.

You may not qualify for a certain policy or it may cost more, if there are other health issues including the cancer after this 6-month window

I have been advised by many healthcare professionals that some of the newest healthcare and cancer procedures are not readily approved by Medicare Advantage plans, but these procedures are generally approved with "Original or Traditional Medicare". They have to fight every day to get the care many desperately need when they have a Medicare Advantage plan. Talk to your medical professional who knows your health situation when making your Medicare plan choice, even if you are someone with a serious health condition, such as heart problems, Alzheimer, MS, end stage renal disease and the list could go on and on…always talk to those that know your health situation

Medicare Advantage HMO NOT Accepted at Nursing Home?

Hello Toni:

My mother has a Medicare Advantage HMO and August 1st she moved into a nursing home in the Sugar Land area. They have a doctor who visits the patients and does not accept the HMO which she has. The nursing home director is advising me to disenroll her from this plan, so my mother can use the facility doctor or else they will have to ambulance her when she needs care

Is there a way that she can make a move because Medicare Open enrollment is not until October? I need to do this ASAP and get her on Original Medicare

I have been following your column and have never seen you address this type of issue. What do I need to do?

Stephanie, a weekly reader

Yes Stephanie:

There is help for your mother and it really is not as hard as you may think.

Typically, I write about ***Special Enrollment Periods*** (SEP) for those who are past 65, retiring and leaving their company benefits, but there is a SEP for those who are moving into institutional care such as nursing homes.

In the Medicare and You Handbook, it talks about the specifics ***Special Enrollment Period*** The Medicare and You Handbook states, "You generally must stay enrolled for the calendar year. However, in certain situations, you may be able to join, switch, or drop a Medicare Advantage Plan during a ***Special Enrollment Period***. Some examples are:

- Moving Out of Area:
- Enrolled in Medicaid

- Qualify for Extra Help for prescription drugs.
- Moving into an institution (like a nursing home) *which your mother qualifies for*
- Loss of creditable prescription drug coverage. (insurance through your employer).

The trick to disenrolling from a Medicare Advantage Plan when a SEP is granted is to enroll in a Stand-alone Part D plan and being able to answer the qualifying question which is that you have moved into that facility within a 2-month period or have moved out of the facility within a 2-month period.

If you wait past the 2-month window, then she will have to wait until Medicare's annual open enrollment period which is from October 15th to December 7th every year

You will need to contact Medicare at 1/800-633-4227 and give the Medicare customer service agent all of your mother's prescriptions and they will enroll her into whichever Medicare Part D prescription drug plan fits her needs. The Medicare representative will ask you for the date she moved into the facility and it must be within that 2-month window

Once Medicare enrolls her into the new Medicare Part D plan, she will be disenrolled from the Medicare Advantage plan and back to Original/Traditional Medicare. This will be effective on the t of the next month

Remember that with Original/Traditional Medicare, she will have a Medicare Part A (*inpatient hospital*) deductible which is $1364 every 60 days or 6 times a year and a Medicare Part B (*medical insurance*) one-time annual deductible which changes each year. Medicare pays 80% and the Medicare beneficiary (your mother) pays 20%. She may qualify for a Medicare Supplement/Medigap Plan if she can answer the health underwriting questions.

Your mother's situation is why a person enrolling in Medicare should consider all of Medicare's options because no one ever knows when a serious illness will strike and they may need serious medical care

Medicare Supplement or Medicare Advantage Which Way Do I Go!!

Dear Toni

What, if any, is the difference between "advantage" and "supplement"?

Thanks, Joseph

Well Joseph:

Choosing between a Medicare supplement and a Medicare Advantage plan can be trying for some. Some go to the doctor a few times a year and some visit the doctor more. What we say at the Toni Says® office is that, "Medicare is no cookie cutter…one size does not fit all!"

First, talk with your doctor or specialist about which option to pick:

1) Medicare with a Medicare Supplement/Medigap and a standalone Part D Medicare prescription drug plan or
2) Medicare Advantage plan with a Part D Medicare prescription drug plan.

Let's discuss the difference in the two types of Medicare options. Medicare and You Handbook explains what is a Medicare Supplement/Medigap or a Medicare Advantage plan. The Medicare and You Handbook does not compare the differences with the plans.

Below are some of the differences of the two plans:

❖ **Medicare Supplement:**

1. A Medicare Supplement works directly with "Original Medicare". Medicare will pay its share of the Medicare-approved amount for "medically necessary" *(new Obamacare buzz words)* covered healthcare costs. Then, your Medicare supplement will pay its share
2. With a Medicare Supplement you chose which doctor, hospital, home health agency, skilled nursing facility, etc. which accepts Medicare assignment for your healthcare. You and your healthcare provider are in control of your healthcare.
3. With a Medicare Supplement/Medigap, you have a monthly premium that may increase the premium rate each year.
4. You may enroll and will pay separately for a "Stand alone" Medicare (Part D) Prescription drug plan.

❖ **Medicare Advantage Plan:**

1. To qualify for the plan:
   a) You must be enrolled in both Medicare Parts A & B
   b) Live in the service area 6 months out of a year
   c) Not have end stage renal disease (kidney dialysis)
2. When you choose a Medicare Advantage Plan, then Medicare pays the insurance company a certain amount every month for your care as long as you are on the plan. Your Part B premium must be paid each month to keep Part B always in effect.
3. When you go to the doctor or visit your pharmacist, you must only use your Medicare Advantage insurance card, not your Medicare (red, white and blue) card.
4. A Medicare Advantage Plan must provide all of your Part A and Part B benefits and some Medicare Advantage Plans have Part D prescription drug plans included. Also has "extra" benefits such as gym membership, etc.

5. A Medicare Advantage Plan may have a zero to low dollar premiums
6. With a Medicare Advantage plan, you may have different co-pays, co-insurances or deductibles to pay and have maximum out of pocket expenses to meet. Most Medicare Advantage plans have preventative/wellness benefits. Insurance companies have learned that if you stay well, you do not use the insurance as much
7. Some Healthcare facilities, like MD Anderson accept few Medicare Advantage plans. Talk to your provider or facility and make sure they accept the Medicare Advantage plan you want to enroll in. Find out if the Medicare Advantage plans, you are researching, are an "in-network" or an "out-of-network" provider. *(This is very important)*

Doctors Not Accepting Medicare Advantage PPO, Need to Return to Traditional Medicare!

Toni

Last year, I made a mistake and changed to a Medicare Advantage PPO because I understood from talking with my friends that this PPO plan was like a Medicare Supplement. I want out!! Most specialists and even the facility that does MRIs are out of network and this is costing me a fortune. I've been advised to return to Traditional Medicare. Is Traditional Medicare different than Original Medicare?

Advise how I can return to Medicare?

Signed...Jeremy from Tulsa, OK

Dear Jeremy:

You will be happy to know that "Original Medicare" and "Traditional Medicare" are the same thing, but the medical profession knows Medicare as "Traditional" Medicare not "Original Medicare".

Medicare Annual/Open Enrollment will be your only time to make that change. And it is simple for you to enroll in Original/Tradition Medicare and a new Medicare Supplement (without having to answer questions) only because this is your first year to be out of your Medicare Supplement or your first year to pick a Medicare Advantage Plan.

Medicare's Open/Annual Enrollment period starts on October 15, and will end at midnight on December 7th (Pearl Harbor Day) every year.

For you to disenroll from a Medicare Advantage company, all you need to do is enroll in a Medicare Prescription Drug plan that fits your needs. You will **automatically** be out of your old Medicare Advantage plan and back to "Original Medicare" with a Medicare Prescription Drug plan; then you can apply for a Medicare Supplement to pick up what Medicare does not pay for.

Concerned you have health issues which can keep you from qualifying with a Medicare Supplement's application? Don't worry; there are protections in place for this type of situation. The Medicare rule from the Medicare and You Handbook is: "If you join a Medicare Advantage Plan for the first time, and you aren't happy with the plan, you'll have special rights to buy a Medigap policy if you return to Original Medicare within 12 months of joining." Medicare rules concerning this issue are in the Medicare and You Handbook

Below are the changes that a Medicare beneficiary can make to their Medicare plans during Medicare Annual Enrollment:

Enroll in a new Part D Medicare Prescription Drug Plan, which automatically disenrolls you from a Medicare Advantage plan.

Enroll in a new Part D Medicare Prescription Drug Plan when you have never been in Part D from the time you have been with Medicare.

- Change from one Part D Medicare Prescription Drug Plan to a new Part D Medicare Prescription Drug Plan.
- Enroll in a Part C Medicare Advantage Plan with Prescription Drugs
- Change from one Part C Medicare Advantage Plan to a new Part C Medicare Advantage Plan.
- Return to Original Medicare and purchase a Medicare Supplement/Medigap and enroll in a Part D Medicare Prescription Drug Plan.
- Return to Original Medicare only and enroll in a Part D Medicare Prescription Drug Plan.
- Return to Original Medicare with no Part D plan.

✍**<u>*Note</u>**: Don't forget there is a penalty for not enrolling in a Part D Medicare Prescription Drug plan when first eligible.

Has the New Medicare Rule Affected Medicare Advantage Plans?

Toni

Last week you wrote about how the MOON (Medicare Outpatient Observation Notice) rule affects "Original Medicare". My husband has enrolled in a Medicare Advantage HMO and I am wondering how this rule will affect his hospital stay

Thank you, Maria from Cleveland, OH

Maria

The MOON rule only affects those who are enrolled in "Original Medicare" with or without a Medicare Supplement. The rule does not affect those enrolled in a Medicare Advantage plan.

A Medicare Advantage HMO plan has its own process on inpatient and outpatient surgery or hospital stay with a referral only system. With a Medicare Advantage PPO plan, there is not a referral process, but the facility or provider must be willing to bill the Medicare Advantage plan.

The <u>Medicare and You Handbook</u> explains what is a Medicare Advantage plan or "Original/ Traditional Medicare" with a Medicare Supplement/Medigap. The <u>Medicare and You Handbook</u> does not compare the differences between the plans as listed below:

❖ **Medicare Supplement:**

1) A Medicare Supplement/Medigap Plan works directly with Original/Traditional Medicare. Medicare will pay its share of the Medicare-approved amount for "medically necessary" covered healthcare costs. Then, your Medicare Supplement/Medigap will pay its share.
2) You chose which doctor, hospital, home health agency, skilled nursing facility, etc. that accepts Medicare assignment. You and your healthcare provider are in control of your healthcare.
3) With a Medicare Supplement/Medigap, you have a monthly premium that may increase the premium rate each year.

4) You may enroll in and will pay separately for a "Stand alone" Medicare (Part D) Prescription drug plan. If you don't enroll in a Part D prescription drug plan at the right time, be aware that there is a Part D penalty assessed when you do finally enroll and that penalty will last as long as you are enrolled in a Medicare Part D prescription drug plan.

❖ **Medicare Advantage Plan:**

a) To qualify for the plan:
   a. You must be enrolled in both Medicare Parts A & B
   b. Live in the service area 6 months out of a year
   c. Not have end stage renal disease (kidney dialysis)
b) When you choose a Medicare Advantage Plan, then Medicare pays the insurance company a certain amount every month for your care as long as you are on the plan. Your Part B must always be in effect
c) When you go to the doctor or visit your pharmacist, you must only use your Medicare Advantage insurance card, not your Medicare (red, white and blue) card.
d) A Medicare Advantage Plan must provide all of your Part A and Part B benefits and some Medicare Advantage Plans have Part D prescription drug plans included
e) With a Medicare Advantage plan, you may have different co-pays, co-insurances or deductibles to pay and have maximum out of pocket expenses to meet.
f) Some Healthcare facilities like MD Anderson accept few Medicare Advantage plans. Talk to your provider or facility and make sure they accept the Medicare Advantage plan you want to enroll in.

Chapter 5
Medicare Part D *(Prescription Drug)*

Even if you do not take prescription drugs, you should seriously consider enrolling in a Medicare Prescription Drug Plan. You are only required to have Part A to be eligible for a Medicare Prescription Drug Plan. Most people enroll in both A and B when they become eligible for Medicare but some will wait until later to get Part B. There are many reasons, such as having group benefits, still working, having VA benefits, etc. Medicare does not force you to enroll in a Medicare Prescription Drug Plan. If you fail to enroll when you are first eligible, you will face a penalty of 1% per month you wait until you decide to enroll. You can only enroll between October 15th - December 7th every year, what Medicare calls the Annual Enrollment Period (aka Open Enrollment). Let's say you wait 3 years or 36 months to enroll in a Medicare Prescription Drug Plan. You will pay a **PENALTY** 36 months x 1% = 36% more for as long as you are on Medicare. Don't wait

EXAMPLES

Liz's Story - Liz signs up for a prescription drug plan at the time she begins Medicare. Her monthly premium is $30.00 (premium amount is an example only)

Ken's Story - Ken waits 4 years, or 48 months, because he never took any medications. Ken's monthly premium would be 48% more for the rest of his life. He would always pay 48% more than Liz.

Dave and Debbie's Story – Dave and Debbie decided they would save their money instead of getting a prescription drug plan. They retired December 31, last year, and have never used medications. Dave had a heart attack at the Memorial Day Parade. He recovered and was discharged home with a beta-blocker prescription. Suddenly Dave and Debbie learned how expensive medication really is. Debbie called a Medicare Prescription Drug Company on June 7th and was told they cannot enroll until October 15th and the Plan would not start until January 1. Debbie also learned they would pay an addition 12% every month because they did not enroll when they were first eligible for Medicare. *(Price of prescription drug plan and names are fictitious)

Rules for Enrolling in a Medicare Prescription Drug Plan

The rules for enrolling in a Medicare Prescription Drug Plan are different than a Medicare Advantage Plan

1. You can enroll in this plan if you only have Part A. (When first enrolled in Part A your 3-month rule applies for Medicare Prescription Drug Plan)
2. You can enroll in a Medicare Prescription Drug Plan if you have both Part A and Part B
3. You must live in the service area
4. You may only switch plans at certain times of the year. This is from October 15 – December 7 of each year called Annual Enrollment Period (aka Open Enrollment)
5. A Medicare Prescription Drug Plan does not cover vaccines, medical supplies or any drug that is covered under Part B
6. One rule that differs from the Medicare Advantage Plan is that the Medicare Prescription Drug Plan does accept individuals with end-stage renal disease (permanent kidney disease).

REMEMBER: Enroll at the Right Time!!!!!

<u>Two Ways to Enroll in a Medicare Prescription Drug Plan</u>

1) ***<u>ENROLL IN A STAND ALONE POLICY</u>*** –There are stand-alone policies available from private insurance companies which can be used with your Medicare supplement or many group plans that do not cover Prescription drugs. *(Make sure to check when using a Medicare Prescription drug plan with a group retirement health plan because many times it will force you off your group plan, if your company is considered a Medicare Prescription Drug provider. Always check with your company's Human Resource Department because every retirement plan has a different rule.)*
   - Many do not enroll in Part B when they receive Part A because they have not retired, they are still working with true company benefits, and they do not need to have Part B. When they retire, they may no longer have Group benefits and lose their creditable company prescription drug coverage. They will have 63 days to enroll in a new Medicare Part D Prescription Drug Plan.

Reader Alert Medicare Part B should be in place prior to losing group retirement benefits. This is **VERY IMPORTANT!!!**

Please make sure that you enroll in your Medicare Part D Prescription Drug plan within **63** days after you lose your group health coverage when you are retiring after you have turned 65. Don't wait 65 or 70 days to enroll in a Medicare Part D plan. I know this is confusing! Enroll in a Part D plan **<u>after</u>** 63 days and you will receive the 1% penalty per month, that goes all the way back to the day that you have turned 65. Medicare bases the 3-month rule when you have turned 65 and enrolled in Medicare **Part A** only at this time. Makes no sense to me, but that's the rule!!

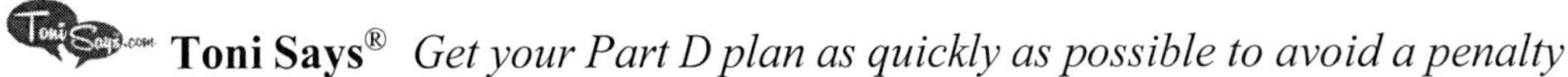

Toni Says® *Get your Part D plan as quickly as possible to avoid a penalty*

2) ***<u>ENROLL IN A MEDICARE ADVANTAGE PLAN WITH PRESCRIPTION DRUGS</u>*** - A MAPD (Medicare Advantage Prescription Drugs) plan includes coverage for hospital, doctor, and prescription drugs, as well as extra benefits that Original Medicare does not offer. All the rules for enrolling are the same with a MAPD plan as with a standalone Medicare Part D plan.

Prescription Drug Tiers:

All prescription drug plans whether stand-alone or MAPD plans have the same number of tier drugs:

<u>Tier 1</u> – **<u>Generic</u>** – covers most generic prescription drugs

<u>Tier 2</u> – **<u>Preferred Brand Name</u>** – Lower Priced Preferred Brand Name prescription drugs.

<u>Tier 3</u> – **<u>Non-preferred Brand Name</u>** – Higher Priced Brand Name prescription drugs.

<u>Tier 4</u> – **<u>Specialty drug</u>** - This includes very rare and experimental drugs. They are generally very expensive medications for serious medical conditions.

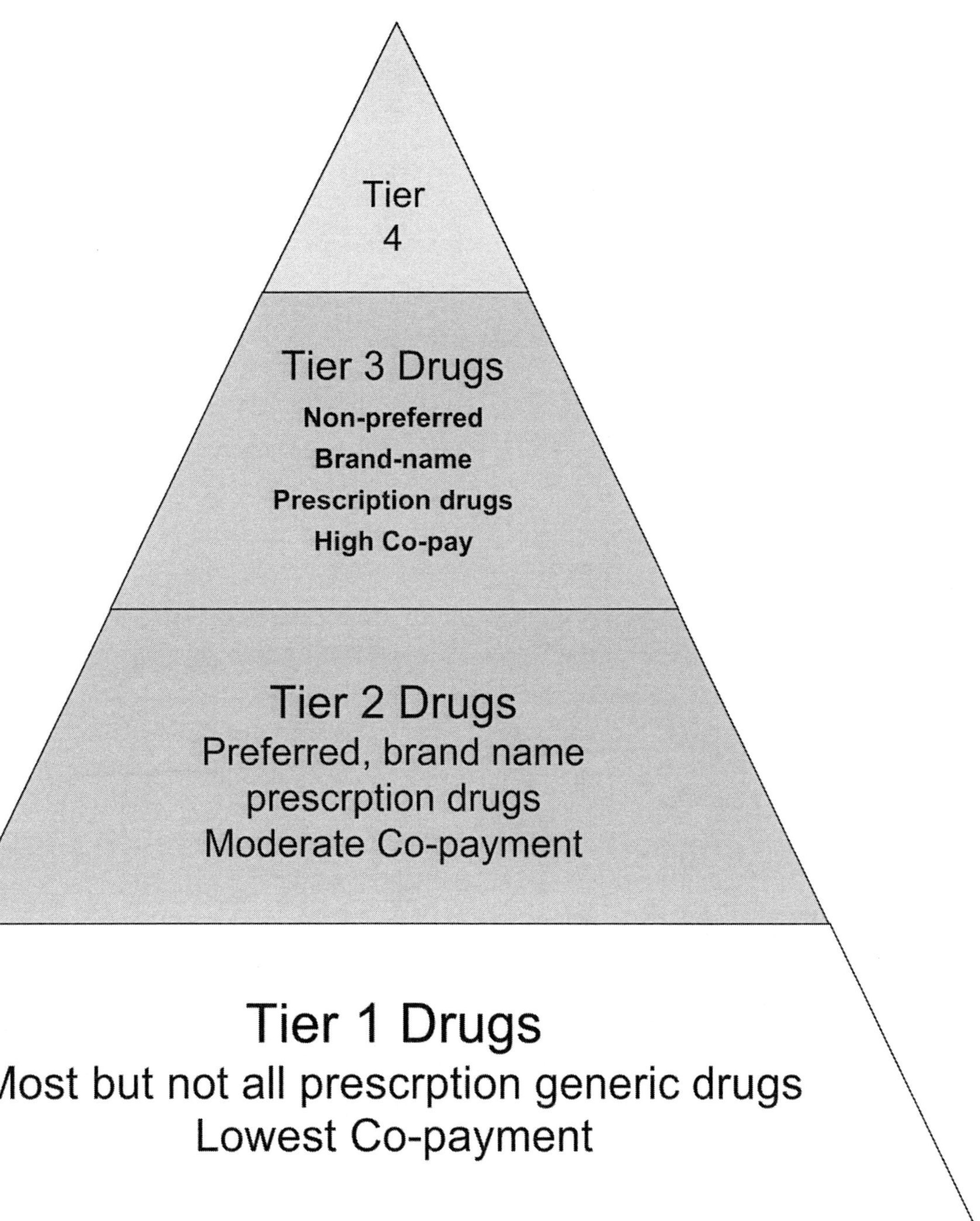

Everyone with a Medicare (Red, White and Blue) card can get Medicare prescription drug coverage, but as I said before, you **MUST ENROLL** or you will have a penalty and will have to pay more when you need it. Even if you only have Part A and not Part B, you can enroll in a Medicare Prescription Drug Plan.

Things to do When Seeking a Medicare Prescription Drug Plan

1. Visit **www.medicare.gov** to compare and find which Part D plan fits your needs.
2. You can only switch plans during Annual Enrollment Period (aka Open Enrollment) October 15 - December 7 every year and your plan will start January 1^{t} You should also visit **www.medicare.gov** to compare plans and benefits.
3. If you need assistance with Part B premiums taken from your Social Security check, the cost of prescription drug premiums and prescription drug co-pays, you may apply for "Extra Help" through Social Security or your local Medicaid office. Visit online at **www.socialsecurity.gov/medicare/prescriptiondrug** help.

Toni Says® *"Many fail to go and ask if they qualify. Nothing ventured... Nothing gained! The worst Social Security or Medicaid can say is No!!*

Different Type of Plans

How the Medicare Prescription Drug Plan works is really very simple and I will "KISS" it (Keep It So Simple) for you to understand.

Exact cost and coverage are different for every Medicare Drug Plan but all plans must offer at least the basic or standard level of coverage set by Medicare. There are 2 different levels of Medicare Prescription Drug Plans that are available to those on Medicare.

1. **The Basic Plan** is the minimal coverage that Medicare allows which includes a premium, a yearly deductible, co-pays or coinsurance, 4 prescription drug tiers and all have the famous "donut hole"/ coverage gap that Medicare changes each year. This is less expensive for you, but has that current year's Part D deductible that is set by Medicare which you must reach each year. If you are not taking very many drugs look in your current year's Medicare and You Handbook that shows what the different plans in your area are and what they cost. The basic plan will get you a Prescription Drug Plan and keep you from the 1% penalty. Medicare does not look at Wal-Mart's $4.00 generic drug plan as creditable coverage, but they do count the VA as creditable coverage.
2. **Enhanced or Preferred Drug Plan** has many different names with different insurance companies in the Medicare and You Handbook and the premiums will vary in price from low to high. They pick up the Standard Medicare Prescription Drug Plan deductible and have the 4 prescription drugs tiers and various co-pays. An enhanced or preferred drug plan is generally the Part D plan that most enroll in because there is no deductible

Both types of Part D whether basic or enhanced/preferred plans have the "famous donut hole" or coverage gap. Many will cover only generics through the "donut hole". To this date, I have not seen any plans cover brand or non-preferred brand names through the "donut hole". The most cost-effective way to handle the high cost of prescription drugs is to use as many generics as possible.

What is the "Donut Hole"?

Each year, the Medicare Prescription Drug Plan has a "donut hole" or coverage gap and as I said earlier, it changes each year. You must spend your true out of pocket cost, which will also changes each year. The "donut hole" begins after the total yearly drug costs including what your drug plan has paid and what you have paid reaches a certain amount which will be defined each year in the Medicare and You Handbook

If you have prescription drug coverage from a Medicare Part D drug plan, at some point during the year, the amount you pay for your prescriptions may suddenly increase. This may be because you have reached the "donut hole (sometimes called the coverage gap). !

Let's use the 2022 figures as an example to explain the "donut hole" which is now called the **"donut hole discount"**. Remember these figures change each year. For 2022, the **donut hole discount"** begins at $4,430. Once you reach the **"donut hole discount"** you will have to pay a certain percentage of the covered brand name drugs. In the 2022 example, you would pay 25% for a covered brand name drugs and will receive a 75% **"donut hole discount"** with the drug company paying 70% and the Part D prescription drug plan pays the remaining 5% and for covered generic drugs you pay 25% until your prescription drug costs total $7,050. January 1st of each year this amount changes for where the "donut hole discount" begins, when your co-pays and what your drug plan have paid until it reaches the catastrophic coverage set amount.

Once the total yearly amount has been spent for the "donut hole discount" then you can use your prescription drug card again and go into Catastrophic Coverage. It doesn't matter what Medicare Prescription Drug Plan you are on; they all have the same rules and the same "donut holediscount"!

If your prescriptions are not in your Medicare Part D formulary, then you will pay 100% of the prescription drug cost. Always verify that your prescriptions are in the Medicare Part D formulary.

What is TROOP (true out of pocket)?

The TROOP (true out of pocket) expense is the true cost of the drug including the co-pay. If your Lipitor has a $30.00 co-pay and your prescription drug plan pays $170.00 to your pharmacist, then the true out of pocket is $200.00 or $170.00 cost + $30.00 co pay = $200.00. For every drug that you buy, these amounts (co-pays + costs of drugs) go to the TROOP (true out of pocket) until it reaches the "donut hole". Once you meet the "donut hole" maximum, you will enter theCatastrophic Coverage and the cost of your drugs will go down considerably. In 2022, genericswill be $3.95 for generics with a retail price under $79 and 5% for those priced greater than $79 and brand-named drugs will be $9.85 with retail price under $197 and 5% for brand-named drugs with a retail price over $197. Every January 1st, these costs will change.

Many on the Medicare Prescription Drug Plan will never get out of the "donut hole", due to the fact it usually happens around September or the last quarter of that year and there is usually not enough time to spend the "donut hole" maximum.

If you are actively using your plan to fill your prescriptions, you must keep track of your drug expenses by reviewing your monthly prescription drug plan "Explanation of Benefits" *(also known as an EOB).* You should receive the "Explanation of Benefits" every month from whatever prescription drug company you have chosen to use. *(If you are not receiving a monthly Explanation of Benefits statement (EOB) from your company then tell them to send you one.*

*This is **very important.**)* The "Explanation of Benefits" will tell you how close you are to the "donut hole".

✍ ***Note:** *Check with your doctor before you make any changes to your health care. They know your health care better and know what is best for you. Do not do anything just at a whim because you can't afford your prescriptions!!!! **REMEMBER Talk to your doctor first!***

The following charts show Mary and Molly's similar health situations. They have similar prescription drugs. Mary gets in the "donut hole" and Molly is able to stay out of it. This is only an example. This will help you, or anyone that helps you with your care, to keep you from paying too much for your prescription drugs and staying out of the "donut hole"/coverage gap.

Mary's Prescription Drug Costs

Condition	Medication	Monthly Copay	Total Drug Cost
Acid Reflux	Nexium 20 mg 1 x daily	$25.00	$140.00
Depression	Zoloft 10 mg 1 x daily	$25.00	$110.00
Diabetes	Avandia 4 mg 2 x daily	$25.00	$165.00
High Blood Pressure	Lisinopril 10mg 2 x daily	$4.00	$15.00
Cholesterol	Lipitor 10 mg 1 x daily	$25.00	$90.00
Monthly Total		**$104.00**	**$520.00**

How Long Does It Take Mary To Get
Into the "Donut Hole"?

	Monthly Copay what Mary paid	Insurance Company Pays	Total Drug Cost
January	$104.00	$416.00	$520.00
February	$208.00	$832.00	$1,040.00
March	$312.00	$1,248.00	$1,560.00
April	$416.00	$1,664.00	$2,080.00
May	$1,050.00	$2,080.00	$3,130.00
June	**$1,430.00 plus**	$3,000.00 **Mary gets in the donut hole**	**$4,430.00**
July	$2,140.00		
August	$2,860.00		
September	$3,390.00	**Mary never gets out of the hole!**	
October	$3,890.00		
November	$4,560.00		
December	$5,560.00		
Mary will never get into catastrophic coverage.			

This Example: "Donut Hole" begins at $4,430 and a total of $7,050 must be paid before Mary ever gets out of the "Donut Hole" for the 2022 example

This is ONLY an example!

Molly takes 1 brand name drug and the rest are generics. Saving her $356 in monthly drug cost toward the "donut hole"/coverage gap and saving her $63 in monthly co-pay. Molly's doctor changed her medications to generics. Molly watched her monthly statements. She avoided getting in the "donut hole" for the year.

Molly's Prescription Cost

Condition	Medication	Monthly CoPay	Total Drug
Acid Reflux	Omeprazole 20 mg 1 x daily	$4.00	$29.00
Depression	Zoloft 1 x daily	$25.00	$101.00
Diabetes	Metformin 500mg, 2 x daily	$4.00	$12.00
High Blood Pressure	Lisinopril 10 mg 2 x daily	$4.00	$12.00
Cholesterol	Simvastatin 20mg	$4.00	$12.00
Monthly Total		**$41.00**	**$164.00**

As you can see, Molly never will get in the "donut hole" because her yearly cost of drugs is $1,968, which is well below $4,430 in our example above and the "donut hole" changes each January 1st. She will only spend $492 in co pays for her prescription drugs this year. As you notice, when you do prescription drug planning, it will make your life less stressful, and you will be happier. When you stay out of the "donut hole" you have more money for bills or get to spend your money on fun things that you like!!

Do Your Own Medicare Part D Prescription Drug Planning…?

It's Simple!!

- Visit **www.medicare.gov** and put all of your prescriptions in the site. You will find which plan meets your prescription drug needs. Also, which plan has the best cost for specific pharmacies? Talk to your doctor about using the generic alternative and ask for a new prescription. Just because your MAPD offers $0 cost for mail order prescription drugs, don't think $0 *(no cost)* goes toward your yearly "donut hole" amount. Whatever the true cost of the generic is goes toward your yearly "donut hole" and draws you closer to the famous "donut hole". Remember the old adage "if it sounds too good to be true, it usually is". Nothing is ever free *(there's always a string or two attached)* !!

Toni Says® Do not do anything without FIRST talking to your Doctor!!!

*✍ **Note:** Use preferred pharmacies to control costs.

Reader Alert By not using a preferred pharmacy, you may pay the total cost of prescriptions.

How to Stay Out of the "Donut Hole"?

Each year the "donut hole" changes, but there are ways for staying out of or not getting in it as fast. Know your prices! There are some tricks to the trade and you have got to get in the game!

-hey are as follows:

- If you have quite a few expensive brand name prescription drugs, you may want to do some prescription drug planning. Do not put all of your prescription drugs on your Prescription drug card. Pay for your generic or less expensive brand name drugs out of your pocket. Why you ask???? Because every drug that goes on the card is counted, not just the co pay that you paid, but the total cost of the drug. If you pay **$5** for generic and the pharmacy charges the Prescription Drug insurance company with **$60**, then **$65** (*$5 + $60 = $65)* is charged against your prescription account, getting you closer to the "donut hole"/coverage gap. Use your plan for your expensive brand names drugs. The true costs of those could be $100 to $300 or more. You would rather pay a small co-pay for them instead of the true cost.
- You should talk with your doctor about generic drug selections. Some brand name drugs are now in generic. Make the switch to generic. Tell the doctor about your prescription drug problem and that you are having difficulty paying for the medications. It is easier to pay $5, than $100. Switch to the less expensive/generic drug, if your doctor says it is okay.
- Pay the generic drug out of your pocket. Just because you have a prescription drug plan does not mean you must use it for every drug.
- Control costs with the 500 generic drugs from Wal-Mart, HEB, Costco etc. are $4 or whatever discount price they charge. Check in your area of the country because many stores that have pharmacies are offering generic drugs at a lesser rate. **Do Not Put** the $4 or discounted generic drug on your Prescription Drug Card! These drugs cost $4 or discounted no matter, if you use a Prescription Drug Plan or not. Don't let the pharmacist or pharmacy employee talk you into using your card if you don't want to. If you are concerned that the generics could cause you to go into the "donut hole", then do not use your Medicare Prescription Drug card for simple generic drugs. To avoid confusion, you might want to use 2 different pharmacies

Example:

Pharmacy 1: You use your Medicare Prescription Drug card for your brand name and any very expensive drugs that can cause you to go into the "donut hole".

Pharmacy 2: You don't give them your Medicare Prescription Drug card for your inexpensive drugs. Purchase the $4 or discounted generic drugs, or any inexpensive or discount drugs, out of your pocket.

*Always let the two pharmacies know all the prescription drugs you are currently taking.

If you should reach the "donut hole"/coverage gap, then put everything on your Medicare prescription drug card at Pharmacy 1, where you are paying for the expensive prescriptions and get out of the "donut hole" as quickly as possible.

- See if your doctor can give you samples of the medication you are taking. This will cost you nothing! Asking your doctor for samples maybe the difference between going in the "donut hole"/ coverage gap or staying out of the "donut hole"/coverage gap.

*__Note:__ What confuses the average person on Medicare is that the total cost of the prescription drug is reported to the insurance company, and they report the total amount to Medicare

Co-pay + Insurance Payment = Total Prescription Cost

- For additional assistance, all of the drug manufactures offer assistance programs. You can contact them for help.

What happens when you get out of the "donut hole"?

When the out-of-pocket expense, for your prescription drugs, is more than the yearly TROOP (true out of pocket) at any time in the year, then you have reached Catastrophic Coverage and your Medicare prescription drug plan will begin covering 95% of your prescription drug cost for the rest of that year.

The cost of your prescription drugs will be a maximum of 5% of the drug cost for brand name prescription drugs, or a minimum amount for generic and brand name drugs. Each year these amounts change. In 2022, the amounts are $3.95 for generics and $9.85 minimum for brand name drugs. But remember, these co-pays change every year, but the maximum is always 5% of the brand name drug cost above $197.

There is no cap or limit on the amount of your prescription drug cost after you have spent what is that year's TROOP (true out of pocket).

Toni Says®: Do everything YOU CAN to stay out of the "donut hole"/coverage gap!!! Last year, only 25% of those on a Medicare prescription drug plan reached the "donut hole"/coverage gap. If those on Medicare Prescription Drug plans had done prescription drug planning, the percentage would have been much less.

This is "YOUR" Medicare Prescription Drug Plan.
Use it wisely and "YOU" take control of it!

2022 Medicare Part D Prescription Drug Coverage

Out of Pocket Expenses

(Example Only)

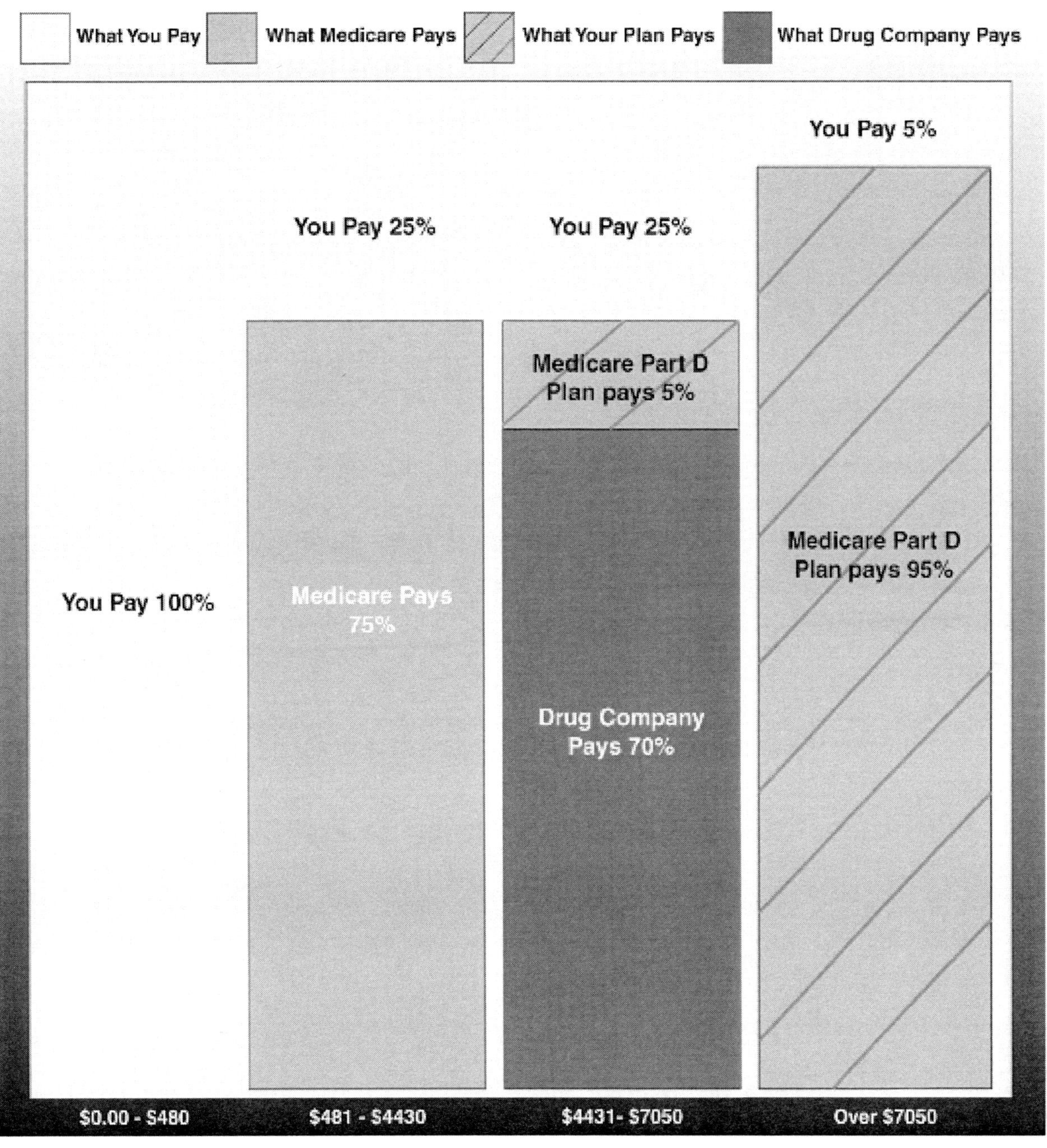

Search through the table of contents for your specific Medicare Part D (Prescription Drug Plan) questions or read the rest of this chapter and gain Medicare Part D (Prescription Drug Plan) knowledge to help yourself or your friends that are confused. Below are articles from the Toni Says® newspaper column regarding specific questions about Medicare Part D (Prescription Drug Plan).

Retiring…Where Should I Focus…

Medicare Health Plan or Medicare Part D Prescription Drug Plan?

Toni

I am retiring January 1st and am beginning to search for the right Medicare option for me and my wife, who is having breast cancer treatment at MD Anderson. Her cancer treatment drugs are semi-expensive and I am concerned about the Medicare Part D out of pocket. I am a diabetic and using the flex pen with high blood pressure prescriptions. Most of mine are generic, except for the diabetic prescriptions

Our Medicare Part B will begin January 1st as my company benefits will end December 31st of this year. What should I do to prepare for this medical insurance change? I will be 70 and my wife is turning 65 by the time I retire, and I want to be sure I do this correctly

Thanks, Dennis from a Katy reader

Great question, Dennis:

The cornerstone of Medicare planning at the Toni Says® office is prescription drug planning. The first topic discussed at a Medicare consultation is what Medicare Part D prescription drug plan or plans **all** your prescriptions. Not all medications are covered under Medicare Part D plans.

Many are concerned about their doctor and completely miss if their prescriptions are covered under their new Medicare Part D or Medicare Advantage prescription drug plan. To their surprise, they must pay 100% out of pocket because their generics or even expensive brand name drugs are not covered

Every Medicare Part D plan has a formulary whether it is a standalone or Medicare Advantage (Part C) with prescription drug plan. If your drugs aren't on that formulary, then you will pay 100% out of your pocket.

When we consult on Medicare at the Toni Says® office, our motto is "Medicare is not cookie cutter… One size does not fit all!" Everyone's Medicare health and prescription drug situation is different and your medical situation as well as the prescription drugs that you take should be considered in your Medicare needs calculation

Those receiving Medicare Part B for the first time need to understand the value of the Medigap (Medicare Supplement) Annual Enrollment Period (aka Open Enrollment). In the Medicare and You Handbook, it discusses "When to Buy" a Medicare Supplement. It states that "the best time to buy a Medigap (Medicare Supplement) policy is during the 6-month period which begins the first day of the month in which you're 65 or older and enrolled in Medicare Part B".

During this 6-month window you can enroll in any Medicare Supplement/Medigap plan without having to answer any health questions and not be denied coverage. After the 6-month window, then medical underwriting takes place and you may not qualify for a Medicare Supplement/Medigap Plan.

At the Toni Says® office, we treat receiving Part B like "gold" because of what it offers

Many new Medicare beneficiaries explore the option of a Medicare Advantage plan which is known as Medicare Part C. It is a good option and with health conditions such as you and your wife have, we advise that you speak with your doctor about what plans they accept or if that provider accepts Medicare Advantage plans.

To explore your options, visit **www.tonisays.com** and sign up for the Toni Says® newsletter, download the Medicare costs, and receive a free copy of the Medicare Prescription Drug Survival Guide e-book version

Take your time and explore your Medicare health and Part D prescription drug options.

America...Is Your Medicare Part B Premium over the minimum amount

Learn How to Lower It!

Toni

A few weeks ago, you wrote about the increases in Medicare's Medicare Part B and D premiums, but you did not explain how to lower your Medicare premiums if my retirement income has lowered

Our joint MAGI (Modified Adjusted Gross Income) in 2013, 2014, and 2015 was approximately $250,000 each year. Once I explained to the local SS office that I was no longer earning the $250K because I had retired, they suggested that we file a Social Security Life Changing Event form

Wham!! Our IRMAA (income related monthly adjusted amount) was reset to zero. My wife and I refile this form yearly to keep our IRMAA at zero because our income now is $75K

Many have income exceeding the IRMAA threshold long after enrolling in Medicare and then their income amount lowers. It would be unfortunate if your readers had no idea that they could pay a lesser IRMAA amount by simply filing a form at their local Social Security office

Your column has helped me understand my Medicare options and I would like to bring help to those that need it. Please explain Social Security's Life Changing Event form...

Another Steve with an IRMAA problem

Thank you, Steve:

You are so right, you can file form titled "Medicare Part B Income-Related Premium - Life-Changing Event" to appeal your Part B/D premium increase if you think your income is lower or not correct. Social Security uses your tax information from two (2) years prior to establish your current income for Part B and D IRMAA premiums.

If your income was more than $91,000 for an individual or $182,000 for a couple, then your Part B/D premiums will be higher than the minimum amount-

Once Social Security is satisfied with the evidence, it will update its records and correct Part B/D premiums to what your current income is. Keep filing the Life-Changing Event form yearly until your income lowers to the basic amount

Don't forget a onetime increase in your income such as property that is sold, cashing in your IRA, or even winning the lottery can change your monthly adjusted gross income (MAGI) that may cause you to pay a higher Part B or Part D premiums.

A life changing event that can change your income can be:

- you have gotten married or divorced, or your spouse has died;
- you or your spouse have stopped working or have reduced your hours;
- you have lost property that you were making money from due to a disaster or other event beyond your control; or
- you or your spouse's benefits from an insured pension plan stopped or went down

Life Changing Event documents to show why your income changed are listed below

You must give the original or a certified copy documents with Life Changing Event form.

If you filed a tax return for the year in which the income-changing event took place, provide a signed copy of your tax return. If you have not yet filed a tax return, you can submit an estimate of the change in your income.
If your marital status has changed, provide a marriage or death certificate.
If your employment status has changed, provide a letter from your employer about your retirement
If you have lost income from a property, provide an insurance claim for property damage.

Part "C" (Medicare Advantage Plan) and Part "D"

(Medicare Prescription Drug) Monthly Premiums

The chart below shows your estimated prescription drug plan monthly premium amount based on your income. If your income is above a certain limit, you will pay an ***income-related monthly adjustment (IRMAA)*** amount in addition to your premium. * The amounts shown are estimates. What you pay may be ***higher or lower*** The Additional prescription drug premium began January 1, 2011

*The income-related monthly adjustment amount (IRMAA) will be deducted from your monthly Social Security check, no matter how you usually pay your plan premium. If the amount is more than your check, you will get a bill from Medicare.

The figure below is used to estimate the Part "D" late enrollment penalty. Part "D" National Base Beneficiary Premium is $33.06;1% Penalty Calculation is $0.3306

If your Yearly Income is File Individual Tax Return	If your Yearly Income is File Joint Tax Return	You Pay
$91,000 or Below	$182,000 or Below	Your Plan Premium
$91,000.01-$114,000	$182,000.01-$228,000	$12.30 + Your Plan Premium
$114,00.01-$142,000	$228,000.01-$284,000	$32.80 + Your Plan Premium
$142,000.01-$170,000	$284,000.01-$340,000	$51.70 + Your Plan Premium
$170,000.01-500,000	$340,000.01-$750,000	$71.30 + Your Plan Premium
Above $500,000.01	Above 750,000.01	$77.90 + Your Plan Premium

Will Medicare Advantage Plan with Prescription Drugs Prevent the "Extra" Part D Premium?

Hello Toni:

I am turning 65 in July, self-employed and my income is over $250K. Recently I received a letter from SSA telling me that my monthly Medicare Part B premium of $134 would be doubled to $267.90 per month due to 2015 reported income. That was no surprise, but Social Security also said that the monthly adjustment for prescription drug coverage would be an additional $34.20. What is this all about?

I am in excellent health and take NO prescriptions. What happens if I do not apply for a Medicare prescription drug plan? Do I still have to pay the "extra" $34.20?

Also - What if a person goes the Medicare Advantage route instead of original Medicare + a supplement? Do they get to avoid the additional $134 per month for Part B and the $34.20 per month for prescriptions?

Thanks, Mike from Oklahoma

Hi Mike

You cannot avoid the additional premiums if your income is above a certain limit

You will have to pay more on your Medicare Part B Medical premium and Part D Medicare Prescription Drug premium when you have enrolled in a Medicare Part D prescription drug plan. If you are not enrolled in a Part D prescription drug plan, whether stand alone or with a Medicare Advantage plan, you will not receive the addition Part D IRMAA (income related monthly adjusted amount) premium.

Social Security bases your income on both you and your spouse whether they are Medicare age or not. The MAGI (modified adjusted gross income) amount that is reported on your yearly income taxes is what triggers the IRMAA increase.

The bottom line is if your income is over these amounts and you have your Medicare prescription drug plan from either a Medicare Advantage (Part C) or Stand-alone Medicare Prescription Drug plan (Part D), you will pay the additional IRMAA premium, whether you are deducting your premiums from your Social Security check or paying direct to Social Security because you have not started taking your Social Security check.

Remember if you are **not enrolled** in a Part D prescription drug plan at the right time, you will not have prescription drug coverage and will receive a Part D late enrollment penalty when you sign up at a later date. At the Toni Says® office, we advise everyone to enroll in a Part D prescription drug plan whether you are taking no prescriptions or a lot of prescriptions. No one wants an additional penalty.

Enrolling in a Medicare Advantage plan instead of Original/Traditional Medicare with a Medicare Supplement/Medigap and a Medicare Part D plan **does not** keep Medicare or Social Security from charging the additional IRMAA premium for both Medicare Parts B and D

The IRMAA Medicare rule went into effect on January 1, 2011, regarding the Medicare Part D additional IRMAA premiums.

Because the Medicare and You Handbooks are generally mailed out before Oct [t], the costs and premiums for that specific year are not included. Medicare costs and premiums are typically released around November 10th of each year.

The readers of the Toni Says® Medicare column can visit www.tonisays.com to receive your copy of the current Medicare costs with Part B and Part D premiums for all income levels and to sign up for the latest Toni Says® newsletter

Current Medicare Benefit/Premium Changes

Hello Toni

I have recently enrolled in Medicare and have received my Medicare and You handbook and cannot find what the Medicare Part A and B deductibles will be? Do you have any idea what the new Medicare costs will be? Why weren't the numbers in the Medicare.gov handbook? Thank You, Sandra from San Antonio, TX

Hello Sandra

Every year the Medicare and You handbook is printed and mailed out before October [t] to all Medicare beneficiaries to help guide them with the Medicare Annual Enrollment period which ends December 7th

The handbook states that at the time of printing the Medicare and You Handbook, the premiums, and deductible amounts for Part A and Part B were not available. Do not know why Medicare cannot include what the new costs will be for next year and with this year being stressful with the new Medicare.gov website change.

But guess what? The Medicare Parts A and B premiums and costs are generally released by the "Centers for Medicare and Medicaid" aka CMS (Medicare) in November and I have some of the cost listed below. Yes, the costs and premiums are changing!!

The 2022Medicare Parts A &B Premiums and Costs Are Below:

- **Part A Costs (Inpatient Hospital)**: The new 2022 Part A inpatient hospital deductible will be an increase from **$1,484** in 2021 to **$1,556 for** 2022, which is an increase of **$72.** Remember the Part A deductible starts over every 60 days. It is not a once-a-year deductible. Under Part A is also Medicare **Skilled Nursing** and your 2022 costs will be days **1-20 $0 copay** per day and days **21-100** will be at **$194.50** per day.
- **Part B Costs (Medical)**: The new 2022 Part B medical/doctor deductible will rise from **$203** yearly deductible to **$233** beginning January 1, 2022, which is a **$30** increase. With Medicare paying 80% of the Medicare approved amount and you (Medicare beneficiary) paying the remaining 20% of the Medicare approved amount.
- **Part B Premiums**: New premium for 2022 will be increased from **$148.50** in 2021 to **$170.10** beginning January 1, 2022. This is an average increase and those with income is higher as an individual or couple will be paying more beginning January 1, 2022.

2022 Medicare Part D costs and copays are explained below:

Part D changes for 2022 are:

- **Initial Deductible:** will be increased by $35 from $445 in 2021 to $480 in 2022.
- **Initial Coverage Limit:** will increase by $300 from $4,130 in 2021 to $4430 in 2022 where the 2022 ***"Donut Hole"*** begins.
- **Out-of-Pocket threshold cost: or (<u>TrOOP</u> true out of pocket)** will increase from $6,550 in 2021 to $7,050 in 2022.
- **Coverage Gap (Donut Hole):** begins once you reach your Medicare Part D plan's initial coverage limit ($4,430 in 2022) and ends when you spend a total of $7,050 out-of-pocket in 2022.
- **Does the Donut Hole really go away?** In 2020, the Donut Hole began being called Donut Hole Discount.
- **What is the Donut Hole Discount:** Part D enrollees will receive a 75% **<u>Donut Hole discount</u>** on the total cost of their **brand-name** drugs purchased while in the Donut Hole. The discount includes, a 70% discount paid by the brand-name drug manufacturer and a 5% discount paid by your Medicare Part D plan. The 70% paid by the drug manufacturer, 5% Part D plan discount combined with the 25% you pay, count toward your TrOOP or Donut Hole exit point.
- **Generic Drug** when one reaches Medicare Part D Donut Hole: pay a maximum of 25% co-pay on **generic** drugs purchased while in the Coverage Gap (receiving a 75% discount).

  For example: If you reach the 2022 Donut Hole, and your generic medication has a retail cost of $100, you will pay $25. The $25 that you spend will count toward your TrOOP or Donut Hole exit point.

Help…My Medicare Nightmare Began with a Letter from CMS about Part D Penalty?

Hello Toni:

I turned 65 in March, I continued to work full time with excellent company benefits, and I decided to delay Part B for 4 years until June 1, when I retired. I enrolled in a Medicare supplement plan G and a Part D prescription drug plan and now the Medicare nightmare has begun?

I have received a notice from CMS (Medicare) saying they do not have record of me having prescription drug coverage that "met Medicare's minimum standards from March 1st when I turned 65 to June 1st when I retired" and I may receive a Part D late enrollment penalty

I thought applying for Part B kept me from a Part D penalty. Can you please advise me what to do? I do not understand any of this!

Thank You, Jonathon, Memphis, TN

Hi Jon

Many retiring after 65, leaving company group health plans and apply for Medicare benefits have to prove they have "creditable coverage" for Part D.

Medicare and You Handbook states

> *"Creditable prescription drug coverage could include drug coverage from a current or former employer or union, TRICARE, Indian Health Service, the VA or health insurance coverage. Your plan must tell you each year if your drug coverage is "creditable coverage". This information may be sent to you in a letter or included in a newsletter from the plan. Keep this information because you may need it when or if you join a Medicare drug plan late."*

The paragraph above, from the Medicare and You Handbook, does NOT advise what creditable coverage is. Creditable drug coverage should "meet or exceed" what Medicare's Part D plan minimums are. The minimum deductible for 2019 should be at least be $415 or less and a maximum out of pocket not more than $5100.00. The benefit amount should be unlimited, so if your plan has a limit or cap it is not credible. Unlimited prescription drug coverage is the key.

Puzzling, I know Medicare does not regard discount prescription drug cards, Wal-Mart, Kroger, HEB or your local pharmacy that offers low cost generics, as "creditable coverage". If you believe these plans can keep you from the Late Enrollment Penalty, I hate to tell you that you're WRONG!! According to CMS (Centers for Medicare and Medicaid Services) these types of prescription drug programs are not creditable at all.

BUT Medicare **DOES** consider receiving your prescription drugs from the VA as creditable coverage. So, the VA is a good option.

Your late enrollment period (LEP) does not begin from the day you lose or leave your company health plan, BUT from the month you turned 65 or began your Medicare and is based on when Part A of Medicare begins not Part B.

This penalty can be because:

A. Your company prescription drug benefits (not health benefits) are not creditable as Medicare declares

B. You simply never enrolled in Medicare Part D when you were first eligible and want to enroll at a later date. Or you wait past the **63 days** without creditable prescription drug coverage when you are leaving company benefits and you are older than 65 years old and 90 days. ***Don't wait past 63 days*** to get Part D when leaving company health plans.

How to Keep the Donut Hole from Getting You!!

Toni

Last year, my mother got into the "donut hole" in October. I can see from the Part D statement she receives that she is rapidly approaching the donut hole and it is only the beginning of May. None of her drugs have changed from the year before

She can afford her co-pays of $180 per month that she pays at the pharmacy. The monthly Part D statement says the prescription drugs' cost is $950 per month. I'm confused

Please give me some ideas to help control this cost!

Thanks, Jennifer from Dallas, TX

Jennifer:

Your mother's prescription drug problem is a typical problem since the cost of brand name prescriptions has risen dramatically. She can afford her $180 co-pays, BUT… has no idea that the true cost of her prescription drugs is $950 each month.

Once her Medicare Part D prescription drug plan and the co-pays she pays total **$4,430** for 2022 for her **covered** drugs, then she is in the famous "Donut Hole" or coverage gap.

She must pay the next $7,050 to get out of the "Donut hole". She will pay 25% for a brand name drug and the brand name drug manufacturer will pay 70% of that covered brand name drug. Now the remaining 5% will be paid by the prescription drug plan which she enrolled in.

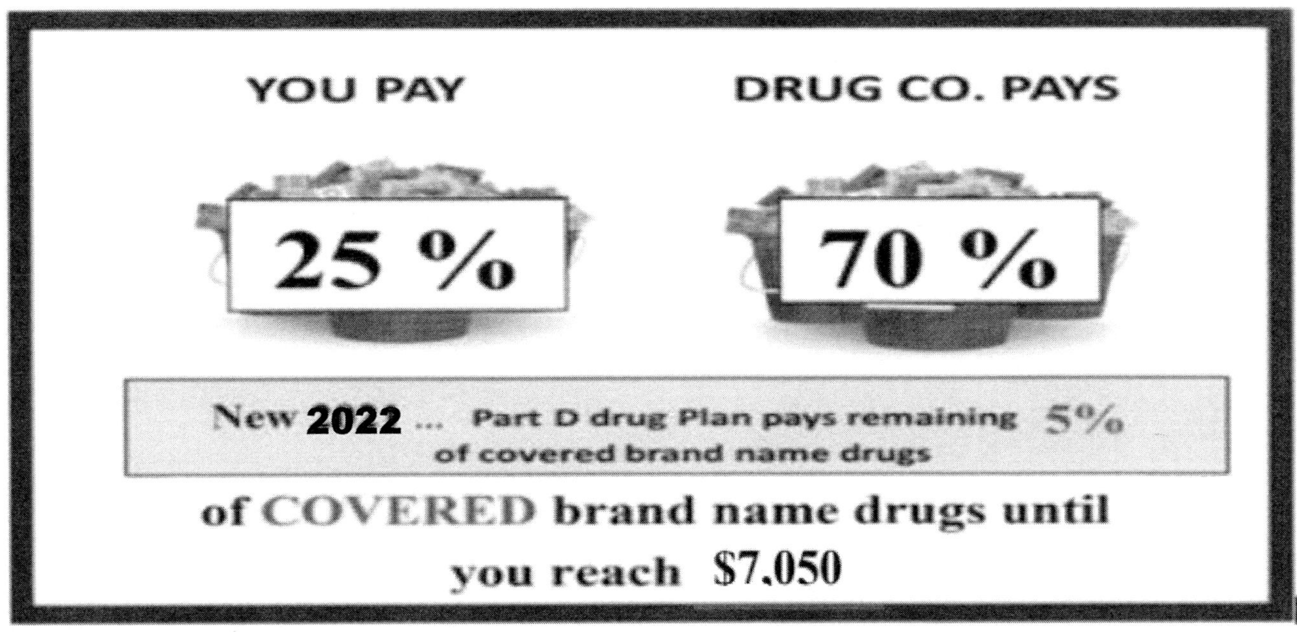

What happens if your brand name drug is not a **"covered"** brand name drug on your specific Part D plan? You will have to pay 100% of that brand name drug.

Generics cost less, but in 2019, the cost was 25% co-pay when in the "Donut hole". Many brand name drugs do not have a generic alternative to use.

That is why it is important when choosing a Medicare Part D prescription drug plan, whether beginning Medicare for the first time or during Fall's Medicare's annual enrollment, to be sure all prescriptions are covered on one's Part D plan.

Do research prior to enrolling in a Part D plan because if you choose the wrong plan, you cannot change it until Medicare's annual enrollment period (aka Open Enrollment), which is from October 15th to December 7th every year

January 1 t of each year, the process starts all over again with a new Medicare Prescription Drug plan and different costs, deductibles, and a new Donut hole.

Toni's Tips to help you stay out of the Donut Hole or not get in it as soon

1) Visit **www.medicare.gov** when selecting a Medicare Part D plan, whether it is your first time or changing during Medicare's Annual Enrollment Period in the f ll. *This is an accurate way toview the cost of drugs and which plan and pharmacy are most cost effective*
2) Talk to your doctor or doctors about which brand name drugs can be changed to generics.
3) Get samples from your doctor.
4) See what generics are in a $4 or $5 generic prescription drug programs at HEB, Wal-Mart, and Costco etc. Pay for the generics out of your pocket. To get their discounted price, you only need a prescription from your doctor.
5) Contact the Prescription Assistance Program in Lake Jackson at 979/285-1430, which has saved over $64 million dollars helping people get their prescriptions at affordable prices when they can't pay for them.

Chapter 6
Medicare Annual Enrollment Period aka...Medicare Open Enrollment

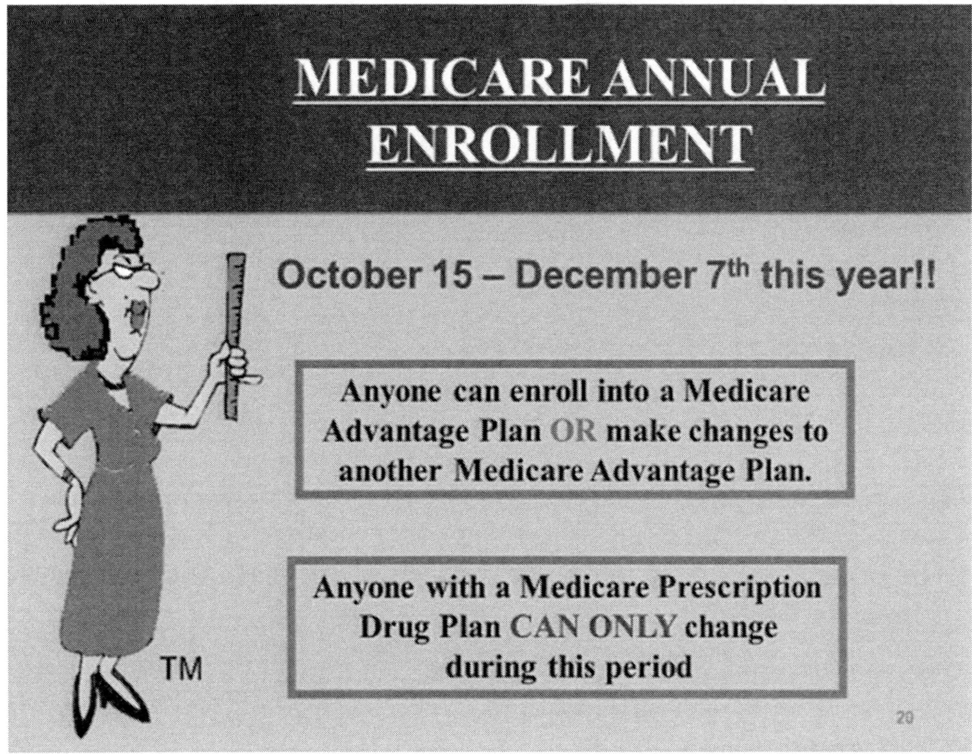

Know Your Enrollment Dates

October 15–December 7th – Annual Election Period (aka Open Enrollment)

Consumers can make a new plan choice. During the Annual Election Period (aka Open Enrollment), any Medicare Beneficiary may elect to join a Part C, Medicare Advantage Plan or Part D Medicare Prescription Drug Plan, for the first time, or switch to a different plan. Any elections made during the Annual Election Period (aka Open Enrollment) become effective January 1 t. During this time, you are able to:

1) Purchase a Part D Medicare Prescription Drug Plan.
2) Change from one Medicare Prescription Drug Plan to a new Medicare Prescription Drug Plan.
3) Enroll in a Medicare Advantage Plan with Prescription Drugs.
4) Change from one Medicare Advantage Plan to a new Medicare Advantage Plan.
5) Return to Original Medicare and purchase a Medicare Supplement and enroll in a Part D Medicare Prescription Drug Plan.
6) Return to Original Medicare and enroll in a Part D Medicare Prescription Drug Plan.

Search through the table of contents for your specific Medicare Annual Enrollment Period (aka Open Enrollment) questions or read the rest of this chapter and gain Medicare Annual Enrollment

Period (aka Open Enrollment) knowledge to help yourself or your friends that are confused. Below are articles from the Toni Says® newspaper column regarding specific questions about Medicare Annual Enrollment Period (Open Enrollment).

Doctor's Not Accepting Medicare Advantage PPO, Need to Return to Traditional Medicare!

Toni

Last year, I made a mistake and changed to a Medicare Advantage PPO because I understood from talking with my friends that this PPO plan was like a Medicare Supplement

I want out!! Most specialists and even the facility that does MRIs are out of network and this is costing me a fortune. I've been advised to return to Traditional Medicare. Is Traditional Medicare different than Original Medicare?

Advise how I can return to Medicare?

Signed...Jeremy from Hockley, TX

Dear Jeremy:

You will be happy to know that "Original Medicare" and "Traditional Medicare" are the same thing, but the medical profession knows Medicare as "Traditional" Medicare not "Original Medicare".

Annual Enrollment Period (aka Open Enrollment) will be your only time to make that change. It will be simple for you to enroll in Original/Tradition Medicare and a new Medicare Supplement/ Medigap (without having to answer questions) only because this is your first year to be out of your Medicare Supplement/Medigap or your first year to pick a Medicare Advantage Plan.

Medicare's Annual Enrollment Period (aka Open Enrollment) period usually starts around, October 15, and ends at midnight December 7. You can find the exact dates in the current Medicare and You Handbook or by going **to www.medicare.gov.**

For you to disenroll from a Medicare Advantage company, all you need to do is enroll in a Medicare Prescription Drug plan that fits your needs. You will **automatically** be out of your old Medicare Advantage plan and back to "Original/Traditional Medicare with a Medicare Prescription Drug Plan; then you can apply for a Medicare Supplement/Medigap to pick up what Medicare does not pay for.

What happens if you have health issues which can keep you from qualifying with the health questions in a Medicare Supplement's application? Don't worry there are protections in place for this type of situation. See the Medicare rules concerning this issue in the Medicare and You Handbook, which states:

> *"If you join a Medicare Advantage Plan for the first time, and you aren't happy with the plan, you'll have special rights to buy a Medigap policy if you return to Original Medicare within 12 months of joining."*

Below are the changes that a Medicare beneficiary can make to their Medicare plans during Medicare Annual Enrollment Period (aka Open Enrollment):

Enroll in a new Part D Medicare Prescription Drug Plan, which automatically disenrolls you from a Medicare Advantage plan.

Enroll in a new Medicare Part D Prescription Drug Plan when you have never been in Part D from the time you have been with Medicare.

- Change from one Part D Medicare Prescription Drug Plan to a new Medicare Part D Prescription Drug Plan.
- Enroll in a Part C Medicare Advantage Plan with Prescription Drugs
- Change from one Part C Medicare Advantage Plan to a new Part C Medicare Advantage Plan. Return to Original Medicare and purchase a Medicare Supplement and enroll in a Part D Medicare Prescription Drug Plan.
- Return to Original Medicare only and enroll in a Part D Medicare Prescription Drug Plan.
- Or Return to Original Medicare with no Part D Plan.

Reader Alert Don't forget there is a penalty for not enrolling in a Part D Medicare Prescription Drug plan when you first become eligible.

Medicare Annual Enrollment Period (Open Enrollment)?

Dear Toni

This is my first Medicare open enrollment, and I don't know anything about this process? Which program is good and which one is not? I do have some health problems and am concerned I am making the correct choice

If you can show me direction and help me, I will really appreciate your help

Thanks Fred from Tulsa Ok

Dear Fred

I am asked this question at least 20 times a week and this is what I tell my clients when they are trying to decide which option is best for their Medicare. Look at the Medicare and You Handbook, it explains the two main Medicare coverage choices; either "Original" Medicare with a Medicare supplement or a Medicare Advantage plan.

To find which Medicare option is best, depends on your individual situation and your health situation. You may be someone who only goes to the doctor once a year or you might be someone who has a long history of health issues. When it comes to a Medicare plan, there is not a one size fits all or a **best** plan. Take your time and search your options.

Here are the 3 steps I use when helping my clients decide which Medicare plan meets their specific needs

Step #1: Decide if you want **"Original/Traditional Medicare" or "Medicare Advantage"** plan.

a) Talk to your doctor and see which plan he/she recommends. Many doctors are accepting "Original/Traditional Medicare" and not Medicare Advantage plans. If you have a doctor that is in the Medicare Advantage plan's provider directory, make sure you call to verify that he/she is still accepting that Medicare Advantage plan. Sometimes providers are in the directory but stopped accepting the plan long before it went to print. The mostaccurate way to check for a provider is from that specific company's website.

a) The main difference between "Original/Traditional Medicare" and Medicare Advantage plans is "Original/Traditional Medicare" works **only** with Medicare and generally, you or your supplemental coverage pays the deductibles or coinsurances
b) A Medicare Advantage plan is also called Part C and is administered by private insurance companies that are approved by Medicare. You must use that insurance company's card not your *Medicare (Red, White and Blue) Card*

Step #2: Decide if you want **Medicare Part D** prescriptions drug coverage.

c) If you want Medicare Prescription Drug coverage to go along with "Original/ Traditional Medicare" then you must enroll in a standalone Medicare Part D plan with a private insurance company that is approved by Medicare and usually there is a premium.
d) If you choose a Medicare Advantage plan, please make sure that the plan has Part D Medicare Prescription Drug coverage included.

Step #3: If you chose "Original/Traditional Medicare, you may want to also select **Medicare supplemental** (Medigap) coverage.

a) A Medicare Supplement/Medigap fills the gap of "Original/Traditional Medicare"
b) You can choose to buy a Medicare Supplement (Medigap) policy from a private insurance company. Cost will vary by policy and company.

✍***Note** You have until midnight the last day of Annual Enrollment Period (aka Open Enrollment) to make your Medicare plan choice which will begin January 1 t. If you miss the deadline, you will have to wait until the next year for Annual Enrollment Period (aka Open Enrollment) to begin again.

ToniSays.com **Toni Says**® Take your time during Annual Enrollment Period (aka Open Enrollment) to change your Medicare options. See other chapters in this book for more on Medicare Supplement and Medicare Advantage.

Under 65 What Should I Do During Medicare Annual Period (aka Open Enrollment)?

Toni

I turn 65 next July, and I'm overwhelmed by all of the mail I am getting this year for Medicare Open Enrollment. What do I do? All the mail from all the companies say theirs's is the best, but they all off the same thing. If I don't do something at the right time everybody says I'll get a penalty that'll last the rest of my life

Matt, Hoover, Alabama

Matt,

Matt…you have to do **NOTHING!!! NADA!!!**

You have no idea how often I am asked this question by those new to Medicare who are absolutely horrified about making a Medicare mistake and receiving a penalty that can last a lifetime. The answer to your question is **NO**…you do not have to do a thing during this year's Medicare's Annual Enrollment Period (aka Open Enrollment) because you are not 65 yet; therefore, you have not enrolled in Medicare yet.

Now next year, Medicare's Annual Enrollment Period (aka Open Enrollment) is when you can make a change to your Part D plan, change, or enroll in a Medicare Advantage plan.

You **MUST** have already turned 65 before Medicare Annual Enrollment Period (aka Open Enrollment) to affect you during this time period.

Since you are turning 65 in July, March is a good time to find out which Medicare option is the right choice for your specific Medicare needs.

As we say in the Toni Says® office, "Medicare is not a cookie cutter, one size or plan does not fit everyone." Although the insurance companies' marketing their specific Medicare plans want you to believe that. Your health and prescriptions needs are not the same as your friends and so you cannot compare your Medicare to theirs.

Toni Says® Medicare Annual Enrollment Period (aka Open Enrollment) is for those who are already 65 and enrolled in a Medicare Plan. You do not have to make a change during the if you enroll in Medicare for the first time that year or are happy with your current plan.

Medicare Annual Enrollment Period (aka Open Enrollment) and Retirement Benefits

Toni

Is there a federal law that I have to change my Medicare? The Toni Says® office helped my husband and me with our Medicare decision in January when James retired from his job of 30+ years and now it seems we have to do this all over again. Could you explain what we need to do?

Everyday our mail box and phone is exploding with people telling me I must make a Medicare change. This is our first Medicare open enrollment experience and I don't want to make the wrong move

Thanks, Sally a West University reader

Sally:

Stress is running rampant this Medicare Annual Enrollment Period (aka Open Enrollment) season because the price of oil is sinking. Texans are concerned that they could lose their jobs or not have enough money for retirement because of a personal healthcare crisis.

There is not a federal law that says you have to make a change to your Medicare. You do not have to change your Medicare Supplement in which you and your husband recently enrolled.

At the Toni Says® office, we advise our clients to always check their Part D plan (go to **medicare.gov**, then go to find health and drug plans and follow the prompts) for any significant changes. If you see a change you should enroll in a new Medicare Part D plan beginning January 1 [t]for the next year.

Below are a few tips to simplify your Medicare Annual Enrollment Period (aka Open Enrollment) or if you are new to Medicare and want to make the best choice you

Have Company Benefits….

Do I Do Anything During Medicare Open Enrollment?

Toni

After speaking with you yesterday, I received a call from my deceased husband's office and was advised that my ex-husband's employer's insurance would expire March 31. He was the principal owner of the company and his (our) deferred compensation and benefits will last until March 31

I am taking the paperwork for Social Security back to their office to get the form filled out correctly with my Part B beginning April 1

I know you have dealt with this and know the ins and outs, but this is all new to me. I need to make sure that I'm processing the paperwork in a timely manner

Does this need to be processed during Medicare Enrollment Period which starts in a few weeks?

Thanks, Sue from Denton, TX

Hello Sue

No, the December 7th deadline does not apply to you because you have employer benefits. This Annual Enrollment Period (aka Open Enrollment) time is for those that want to change or enroll in a Medicare Part D prescription drug plan or to change their Medicare Advantage plan or enroll in another plan.

I know that this is a very stressful time for you because your dear husband handled all of your insurance and financial affairs and you now have to handle life's curves by yourself.

We have been advising those confused by a complicated system, how to enroll in Medicare when they are turning 65, past 65 who have either lost their job because they retired, have been laid off, or have had the "working spouse" pass away and now they have lost company benefits

When we perform a Medicare planning consultation at the Toni Says® office for someone, whether just laid off, retiring or have a loved one who was the "working spouse" pass away, I always advise them to make sure that they have their Part B in place when leaving their employment and/or group benefits.

The process to enroll in Part B, when you are past 65 must be done correctly:

- Call Social Security at 1/800-772-1213 and advise them that you have left your company, are retiring or lost benefits due to the death of a spouse and need to enroll in Medicare Part B because you had delayed Part B. They will send you 2 forms:
    - **Form # 1 Request for Employment Information:** proof of group health care coverage based on current employment. If you have had 2 or more jobs since turning 65, then all companies you or your spouse have worked for from age 65 to the time you or your spouse are retiring, to sign this form. If you are married, you will need the same number of forms filled out for your non-working spouse and signed by the companies HR departments for which you or your spouse has worked, proving the non-working spouse was covered by company insurance (if the non-working spouse is Medicare or Medicare eligible) On the top of each form write in ***red letters "Special Enrollment Period".***

Below is a Sample of what the form looks like.

Special Enrollment Period

DEPARTMENT OF HEALTH AND HUMAN SERVICES
CENTERS FOR MEDICARE & MEDICAID SERVICES

Form Approved
OMB No. 0938-0787

REQUEST FOR EMPLOYMENT INFORMATION

SECTION A: To be completed by individual signing up for Medicare Part B (Medical Insurance)

1. Employer's Name
2. Date __/__/____
3. Employer's Address

City | State | Zip Code

4. Applicant's Name
5. Applicant's Social Security Number ___-__-____
6. Employee's Name
7. Employee's Social Security Number ___-__-____

SECTION B: To be completed by Employers

For Employer Group Health Plans ONLY:

1. Is (or was) the applicant covered under an employer group health plan? ☐ Yes ☐ No
2. If yes, give the date the applicant's coverage began. (mm/yyyy) __/____
3. Has the coverage ended? ☐ Yes ☐ No
4. If yes, give the date the coverage ended. (mm/yyyy) __/____
5. When did the employee work for your company?
   From: (mm/yyyy) __/____ | To: (mm/yyyy) __/____ | Still Employed: (mm/yyyy) __/____
6. If you're a large group health plan and the applicant is disabled, please list the timeframe (all months) that your group health plan was primary payer.
   From: (mm/yyyy) __/____ | To: (mm/yyyy) __/____

2. **Form #2 Application for Enrollment in Medicare** *(a sample copy is below and again in the Forms section)* this is you and your spouse's application for medical insurance from Medicare known as Part B. Social Security fills out this form. Also on the top of each form write in ***red letters "Special Enrollment Period".***

Below is a Sample of what the forms looks like.

DEPARTMENT OF HEALTH AND HUMAN SERVICES
CENTERS FOR MEDICARE & MEDICAID SERVICES

Form Approved
OMB No. 0938-1230

APPLICATION FOR ENROLLMENT IN MEDICARE PART B (MEDICAL INSURANCE)

1. Your Social Security Claim Number ___-__-____ | Beneficiary Identification Code (BIC)
2. Do you wish to sign up for Medicare Part B (Medical Insurance)? ☐ YES
3. Your Name (Last Name, First Name, Middle Name)
4. Mailing Address (Number and Street, P.O. Box, or Route)
5. City | State | Zip Code
6. Phone Number (including area code) (___) ___-____
7. Written Signature (DO NOT PRINT)
   SIGN HERE
8. Date Signed __/__/____

IF THIS APPLICATION HAS BEEN SIGNED BY MARK (X), A WITNESS WHO KNOWS THE APPLICANT MUST SUPPLY THE INFORMATION REQUESTED BELOW.

9. Signature of Witness
10. Date Signed __/__/____
11. Address of Witness
12. Remarks

- A "***Special Enrollment Period***" (SEP) lasts for an 8-month period. During that 8-month time, if you don't enroll in Medicare Part B and you have a medical emergency or simply need to go to the doctor, you will be without any of the advantages that Part B provides and you will bear the cost of your doctor services, etc. 100% out of your pocket. Enroll after the 8-month window and you will receive a Part B penalty which goes all the way back to the day you turn 65. If you get sick and have not enrolled in Part B, you may not have any of the benefits Medicare Part B provides.
- Once you have Parts A and B in place, then you can make your choice for a Medicare Supplement and a Part D prescription drug plan or a Medicare Advantage plan.

✍*<u>Note</u>:** When you receive the Request for Employment Information form, make sure you write in **RED ink** across the top of the form "***Special Election Period***" (if it is not written on the top of the form in red, then you write it using red ink). Take it to the HR department. they must fill it out and sign the form. Now, you are ready to get off your company benefits. Take both forms to your local Social Security office for your Medicare Parts A/and B to begin.

Laid Off…Enrolled in Medicare

Why is My Part B Premium Over $400?

Dear Toni

I lost my job in December when the oil prices began to tank. I was an engineer and 2 years ago my income, which Medicare used to determine my Part B premium, was over $300,000

Today I received a letter from Social Security stating that I must pay $389.80 for Part B and $72.90for Part D, totaling over $402.00 monthly from my Social Security check

I was recently told that you understand the Medicare rules and I could possibly appeal my Medicare premium because I am not working full-time with an income of $300,000; instead, I'm only receiving a $2,400 monthly Social Security check

What do I do to appeal this decision and bring my Medicare premium to a lower, affordable amount?

Thanks…Guy from Hockley, TX

Mr. Guy:

I hear about this Part B and D premium problem almost every day since companies have been laying off higher-income older employees. People think that everyone pays the same amountfor their Medicare Parts B and D, but those days are long gone. If your income for an individual is over $91,000 (or married is over $182,000); your Parts B and D premiums will be more.

Social Security explains how they arrived at the Part B and D premiums based on your "Modified Adjusted Gross Income" (MAGI) from your last filed tax return.

In your case, your MAGI was over $300,000 and the table used in the letter you received from Social Security shows what the Part B and Part D premium adjustment *(nice way of saying it's going to cost you more)* will be, whether you are filing single or married.

Most retirees do not realize that they have **special situations** also known **as life changing events** that can lower your "income related monthly adjusted amount" (IRMAA).

Below are a few of the life changing events that can make your income go down:

- You have gotten married or divorced, or your spouse has died;
- You or your spouse have **stopped working** or have reduced your hours;
- You have lost property that you were making money from due to a disaster or other event beyond your control; or
- You or your spouse's benefits from an insured pension plan stopped or went down.

If your income has gone down, **YOU** must inform Social Security the month when your Part B is in place or before the end of September of each year, so Social Security can correct your amount to begin January 1 [t] of the next year.

Use the form "Medicare Part B Income-Related Premium - Life-Changing Event" and attach the original documents or certified copies to verify your change in income

Once Social Security is satisfied with the evidence, they will update their records and correct Part B and Part D premiums to what your current income is.

Don't forget a onetime increase in your income such as property that is sold, cashing in your IRA or even winning the lottery (aren't we wishing for that) can change your monthly adjusted gross income (MAGI) which may cause you to pay a higher Part B or Part D premiums

**Social Security reviews your income each year and will adjust your Part B and D premiums to your new income level the next year.

For those interested in the different income levels for Medicare Parts B and D, visit www.Tonisays.com to receive your copy of the current Medicare costs and to sign up for the latest Toni Says newsletter.

Notes

Chapter 7
Rules Not Common to Medicare

Fact 1: Medicare Facts Every Baby Boomer Should Know!

Toni

I am a confused Baby Boomer who needs to make my Medicare decision when I turn 65. I do not know where to start or what to do?

Can you please help simplify this ordeal?

Thanks, Brenda from Tulsa, OK

Brenda

Don't feel alone because those who are entering the maze of Medicare are completely stressed with what their Medicare options are because they know that one wrong move can jeopardize their 401K they worked so hard for and it is all they have left for their retirement days.

Let's discuss a few basic facts that every Baby Boomer should know about Medicare

1) **Enroll on time** The only way Medicare is automatic for those turning 65 is when one is already receiving their Social Security check. If you are not receiving your Social Security check and not working full time with true company benefits, from either you or your spouse's work, then you will want to enroll in Medicare Parts A and B via online at www.socialsecurity.gov/benefits/medicare. Those working full-time with true company benefits or who are covered under their spouse's benefits may want to delay enrolling in Medicare Parts A and B until they finally retire or happen to be laid off from their current employment.
2) **Learn Medicare's alphabet soup, Parts A, B, C & D:** Medicare Parts A and B cover hospital, medical and provider expenses and are referred to as "Original/Traditional Medicare" (the healthcare professionals refer to it as "Traditional Medicare") Medicare Part C known as Medicare Advantage plan is another way of receiving your Medicare benefits. Part D is Medicare Prescription Drug plans that can be enrolled as a stand-alone plan and a Medicare Supplement with Original/Traditional Medicare or bundled in a Medicare Advantage plan.
3) **Medicare covers a lot:** Medicare Part A covers in-patient hospital, skilled nursing facility care, home health and hospice care. Medicare Part B covers physicians' services, outpatient surgery/services, lab/X-rays, MRIs, durable medical equipment and preventative services, etc.
4) **Medicare doesn't cover:** Medicare doesn't cover everything that you want it to cover. Services not covered are vision, hearing, or dental expenses as well as Long-Term Care and basic at in-home assistance
5) **Medicare is NOT free:** Medicare covers a lot and there is a cost associated with Medicare Parts A and B. You have been paying tax dollars for Medicare and the premium for Part A are at no cost because you have paid into the tax system if you have worked 10 years or 40 quarters. Medicare Part B has a premium which is means tested depending on how much you have earned for that year. These premiums change every year. Two Parts of Original Medicare are Medicare Parts A

and B which have a maximum out of pocket expenses that you must meet each year. Medicare Part A (hospital) deductible is not once a year but is every 60 days or 6 times a year. Medicare PartB's deductible changes each year with Medicare paying 80% of the Medicare approved amountand you paying the remainder 20%.

When you visit the Toni Says® office for a Medicare consultation, we tell individuals to forget everything they know about their old health insurance plans because Medicare is totally different!

Toni Says® Baby Boomers are accustomed to a certain type of healthcare lifestyle and for someone who is new to Medicare it can be an eye-opening experience. Take your time, when retiring and leaving medical benefits whether leaving true group benefits or being self-employed with individual health insurance. Medicare is a new change. Take some time when making choices foryou and/or your spouse's Medicare choices. Remember there are no do-overs when it involves your Medicare decisions

Fact 2: Not Knowing Medicare Rules Costs Americans Millions!

Toni

Recently, we sold our house to move into a senior community. Now, both of our Part B premiums have increased drastically from the average monthly amount for each month to the maximum amount one can pay each month for Part B and an additional increase for Part D. We still are receiving the same Social Security check and I really don't understand where this change came from

Could you please explain what has happened?

Meredith from Myrtle Beach, NC

Meredith

In the past few weeks, when clients are meeting with us at the Toni Says® office, we are seeing those on Medicare who do not fully understand the Medicare rules.

Below are a few examples of how Americans are paying more for Medicare Part B and Part D premiums:

. **Part B and D monthly premiums are based on what income amount was reported on your last filed tax return:** Meredith, your question about why your Part B and D premiums increased even though your Social Security checks remained the same, tells me that your income for that year was raised from the year before. When you and your husband filed jointly and your income on your joint tax return was $182,000 or less you paid the lowest Part B premium. Because of the amount, you received from the sale of your home, it raised your income for last year. In turn, your Parts B and Part D, which are means tested, increased as a result of what was declared on your last tax return. Medicare Beneficiaries need to know, when your income increases above the threshold of $91,000.01 as an individual or $182,000.01, as a couple, both your Parts B and D premiums will be increased accordingly.

2. **Should one enroll in Medicare Part B when either you or your spouse is "still" working with employer health coverage?** Everyone should discuss enrolling in Part B with their company' HR or benefits administrator to find out how their group health coverage coordinates with

Medicare. It may be to you or your spouse's advantage to delay Medicare Part B. The Medicare and You Handbook states, "You can sign up for Part B without paying a penalty anytime you have health coverage based on you or your spouse's current employment." Once employment or health coverage based on employment ends, then you can receive a SEP (***Special Enrollment Period***) and have an 8-month period to enroll in Part B without receiving a Part B penalty. When someone has been enrolled in Medicare Part B for longer than 6 months, Medigap (Medicare Supplement) open enrollment will not exist and you may not qualify for that specific Medicare Supplement plan because now you must answer health questions.

3. **Each employer's HR Department will need to complete and sign the Social Security form "request for employer information" when there is an employment change past turning 65?** One of our clients consulted a Toni Says® agent regarding enrolling in Part B when leaving their current employment only to discover that they never had two (2) other companies (which she had worked for after turning 65) sign the form #QMB No. 0938-0787, Request for Employment Information. The earlier mentioned client was now 69, so they received a Part B penalty because they did not have all of the previous companies they were employed by, sign the forms. The penalty will be 69 minus 65 which is 4 (full 12-month periods) times 10% or 40%. Not for one month, but for as long as they are enrolled in Medicare Part B. If your spouse is being carried on your company insurance and is 65 or older, you must also have the HR department of each company you worked for, fill out the Request for Employment Information for your spouse to prove your spouse was covered by your company insurance, so they will not receive a penalty when they enroll for Medicare Part B

Toni Says® Above are 3 simple Medicare and Social Security rules which the average person is not familiar with. Social Security monitors your yearly income from what the IRS informs them and can change your Part B premium when notified that you have had an income increase for that year. Also, Social Security is the gate keeper when someone is leaving company benefits and needs to enroll in Medicare Part B without being charged a Part B penalty. Learning the 3 rules above can save you and your spouse some heart ache and frustration.

Fact 3: Can't Afford to Pay My Medicare Premium Bill…

What Can I Do? Medicare easy pay

Toni

My Medicare begins June 1st and I have received my first bill. This bill is for 4 months from June st to September 30th. I thought Medicare was monthly. If I pay this amount, then I cannot pay my rent for June

This bill for Medicare is due June 25th and I was wondering if Medicare allows payments for Medicare Part B premiums on a monthly basis? I can't start my Social Security check because I work and make more than Social Security allows without having to pay a penalty because I am not at my full retirement age (FRA)

Jackie, Natchitoches, La

Jackie

Most that are paying their Medicare premiums monthly have the premium taken from their Social Security check. Social Security will automatically take the Medicare premiums from a person's Social Security check. Social Security will send a letter informing the Medicare beneficiary that Social Security is deducting the monthly Medicare Part B premiums from your Social Security check.

Many are not receiving a Social Security check because they are still working full time and make more than the annual allowable amount. When someone does make more than allowed (the allowed amount of monetary compensation received each year is subject to change), they will have to pay $1 for every 3 dollars earned. Once the Medicare Beneficiary reaches Full Retirement Age, Social Security says there is no cap on how much you make.

The least Medicare Part B premium for those who income is $91,000.01 or less as an individual or $182,000.01 or less as a couple is set each year by the U.S. Government, and is subject to change, depending whether or not those on Medicare received a cost of living raise to their Social Security check.

GOOGLE "Medicare easy pay" or go to www.medicare.gov and you can research different topics, including how to pay Medicare Parts A, B, C and/or D, how to set up Medicare Easy Pay or download the form/s you will need to pay monthly.

For those who do not have access to a computer, call 1/800-MEDICARE (633-4227) and request for the "Medicare Easy Pay" form to be sent by mail to you.

If you do not keep up with your Medicare premiums, whether it is Part A, B, C and/or D, then the Medicare Beneficiary might lose their benefits and may be charged a penalty when they re-enroll. (When someone does not have the required 40 working quarters to qualify for Medicare, then they may also have to pay a premium for Part A.)

It may take about 6-8 weeks to have the "Medicare Easy Pay" form processed. You should make sure that you keep up with your monthly premiums, so your Medicare Parts A, B, C and/or D are kept on a current basis.

Toni Says® Many do not realize that they can pay their Part B premiums monthly when not receiving their Social Security check but must follow the rules set up by Medicare. Take your time and study this Medicare rule.

Fact 4: Learn the Myths of Medicare

Toni

I have been following your "Toni Says®" Facebook page and last week you had a chart discussing different myths of Medicare. It seems I am just as confused as those taking the survey

I have recently been diagnosed as having Parkinson's and want to be sure I make the correct choice

I do not understand why I need to enroll in Medicare, since I have excellent company retirement health insurance

John

Hello John

Below is my response to the myths from the Facebook page:

Myth #1 A person can enroll in Medicare any time after they're 65 without penalty FALSE!! This idea is wrong. If you are not working fulltime for a company with true group benefits and wait later than 65 years old and 90 days to enroll in Part B, then you can receive a penalty of 10% for each 12-month period or year that you did not enroll in Part B. That penaltylasts for the rest of your life.

John since you are not working fulltime for the company you have retirement benefits with, I would advise you to enroll in both Medicare Parts A and B to keep from receiving the late enrollment Part B penalty later.

Toni Says® If you or your spouse are not working fulltime with true company benefits be sure to enroll in Parts A and B by the time you turn 65. Wait 90 days past turning 65 and you will get a penalty

Myth #2: Medicare is free. FALSE!! The Medicare payroll tax that you have been paying for years is for Medicare Part A only! Part B has a premium which is means tested due to your income and your spouse's income (if you filed jointly). Most on Medicare are paying the minimum required each month for Part B, but 10% of Medicare Beneficiaries meet the means tested income amount and must pay more for their Medicare Part B premiums each month. If you do not pay the Part B premium, you will not have any of the Part B benefits.

Toni Says® Nothing is free!! You worked and paid taxes into the Social Security system

Myth #3: Most baby boomers think Medicare is just like regular health insurance plans. FALSE! Medicare is completely different than traditional group or individual health insurance. Medicare has two Parts A & B. Part A has a deductible that can be charged up to 6 times a year for an inpatient hospital stay (depending on how many times you are admitted to the hospital). Medicare Part B includes doctor's services such as office visits and doctor performing surgery, outpatient services and surgery, scans, x-rays, chemotherapy and radiation, wheelchairs, walkers and the list goes on. There is a deductible for Medicare Part B that is a once per year deductible, with Medicare picking up 80% and you pay 20% of the Medicare approved charges, with no co-insurance or stop loss. Not like the typical 80/20 to $5,000 with a stop loss, that most have been familiar with most of their adult life. With Medicare the 20% just keeps on going!? **That'scorrect, no stop loss!**

Toni Says® Medicare is completely different than health insurance. The out of pocket can be huge. Learn about the different Medicare plan options to pick up your out-of-pocket costs.

Myth #4... Medicare covers everything. FALSE Most baby boomers are surprised to find out that Medicare does not cover long term care, routine dental care, dentures, cosmetic surgery, exams for hearing or hear aids and acupuncture. Medicare only covers what is **medically necessary**

Toni Says® Medicare will only pay for medical expenses and if Medicare doesn't pay, then your Medicare supplement or Medicare Advantage plan will not pay either

Fact 5: Medicare Open Enrollment Options?

Dear Toni

This is my first Medicare open enrollment and I don't know anything about this process? Which program is good and which one is not? I do have some health problems and am concerned I am making the correct choice

If you can show me direction and help me, I will really appreciate your help

Thanks Fred from Tulsa Ok

Dear Fred

I am asked this question at least 20 times a week and this is what I tell my clients when they are trying to decide which option is best for their Medicare. Look at the Medicare and You Handbook, it explains the two main Medicare coverage choices; either "Original" Medicare with a Medicare supplement or a Medicare Advantage plan.

To find which Medicare option is best, depends on which option is best for your health situation. You may be someone who only goes to the doctor once a year or you might be someone who has a long history of health issues. When it comes to a Medicare plan, there is not a one size that fits all or a **best** plan. Take your time and search your options.

Here are the 3 steps I use when helping my clients decide which Medicare plan meets their specific needs

Step #1: Decide if you want **"Original Medicare"** **"Medicare Advantage"** plan.

Talk to your doctor and see which plan he/she recommends. Many doctors are accepting "Original Medicare" and not Medicare Advantage plans. If you have a doctor that is in the Medicare Advantage plan's provider directory, make sure you call to verify that he/she is still accepting that particular Medicare Advantage plan. Sometimes providers are in the directory, but stopped accepting the plan long before it went to print. The most accurate way to check for a provider is from that specific company's website.

b. The main difference between "Original Medicare" and Medicare Advantage plans is "Original Medicare" works **only** with Medicare and generally, you or your supplemental coverage pays the deductibles or coinsurances
A Medicare Advantage plan is also called Part C and is administered by private insurance companies that are approved by Medicare. You must use that insurance company's card not your *Medicare (Red, White and Blue) Card*

Step #2: Decide if you want **Medicare Part D** prescriptions drug coverage.

a. If you want Medicare Prescription Drug coverage to go along with "Original Medicare" then you must enroll in a standalone Medicare Part D plan with a private insurance company that is approved by Medicare and usually there is a premium.
b. If you choose a Medicare Advantage plan, please make sure that the plan has Part D Medicare Prescription Drug coverage included.

Step #3: If you chose "Original Medicare you may want **Medicare supplemental** (Medigap) coverage.

a. Medicare Supplements fill the gaps of "Original Medicare".
b. You can choose to buy a Medigap/Medicare Supplement policy from a private insurance company. Cost will vary by policy and company.
c. You have until Sunday, December 7th to make your Medicare plan choice to begin January 1 of that year until Medicare Open Enrollment which begins on October 15th of that year.

Toni Says® Take your time during Medicare Open Enrollment in the fall to change your Medicare options. More on Medicare Supplement and Medicare Advantage in these chapters.

Fact 6: Under 65 What Should I Do During Medicare Open Enrollment?

Toni

I turn 65 next July, and I'm overwhelmed by all of the mail I am getting this year for Medicare Open Enrollment. What do I do? All the mail from all the companies claims theirs is the best, but they all offer the same thing. If I don't do something at the right time everybody says I'll get a penalty that'll last the rest of my life

Mike, Birmingham, Alabama

Mike,

You have no idea how often I am asked this question by those new to Medicare who are absolutely horrified about making a Medicare mistake and receiving a penalty that can last a lifetime. The answer to your question is **NO**...you do not have to do a thing during this year's Medicare's open enrollment because you are not 65 yet. You have not enrolled in Medicare yet

Now next year, Medicare's open enrollment period is when you can make a change to your Part D plan or change or enroll in a Medicare Advantage plan.

You **MUST** have already turned 65 before Medicare open enrollment for this time period to affect you.

Since you are turning 65 in March now is a good time to find out which Medicare option is right choice for your specific Medicare needs.

As we say in our office, "Medicare is not cookie cutter...one size or plan does not fit all." Although the insurance companies marketing their specific Medicare plans want you to believe that. Your health and prescriptions needs are not the same as your friends and so you cannot compare your Medicare to theirs

Toni Says® Medicare is for those who are already 65 not for those that are just turning in a few months. Why would one have to make a Medicare option if they are not turning 65 and enrolled in Medicare

Fact 7: Myth or Fact…I'm Losing My Retirement Insurance

Hello Toni

This fall, my retiree insurance from ATT was cancelled and my husband and I are no longer covered under the ATT company plan. I am afraid that my husband and I are not going to be taken care of since we were forced to make this change

Can you please explain a few of the stories that I have heard? Mainly, doctors are not accepting Medicare and that if you are over 75 and need care for cancer, that it will be denied

I have heard that these changes are because of Obamacare. Please tell me what is true and what is a rumor?

Thanks, Anne from Georgetown, TX

Hello Anne,

Never have I seen the Medicare community as concerned about Medicare or their healthcare as they are now, since many corporations such as AT&T, Baker Hughes, CITGO, IBM, and many other companies have let their retirees go to search for new Medicare plans.

Last April 1, Marathon Oil released their retirees from their group health plan. I would say that the year is starting off with a bang!

One thing the Affordable Care Act or Obamacare is affecting, is how your Medicare dollars are being spent.

Below are some of the myths and facts that are circling around in the forms of a bogus email that we all are getting.

Doctors will not be accepting Medicare because of healthcare reform. *This is a fact* anda tricky one Many of your "smaller" family clinics that do not specialize in the 65 or older community, are not processing Medicare claims and thus not accepting Medicare assignment but there are plenty of primary care physicians or PCPs that are still accepting Medicare patients. Larger clinics are generally still accepting Medicare as well as Medicare Advantage plans. For those turning 65 soon, make sure to establish a relationship with a primary care physician as well as a specialist prior to turning 65. Do not wait until the last minute to start going to the doctor because it may be hard to find one that is accepting **"NEW"** patients. Many doctors are accepting current patients for Medicare with no problems but have what is called a **"closed panel"** for new patients.

If you are over 75 and on Medicare, you will be denied cancer treatment! This is a myth. Medicare does not distinguish what age you are as to what treatment you will receive. If it is "medically necessary" then Medicare will pay for it. Medicare does not ration care because of age.

Due to Obamacare, a patient must be admitted in the hospital by their primary care Physician not an ER doctor for Medicare to pay: This is a myth. Medicare will pay, but the claim must be classified as "formally admitted" for Medicare Part A, in hospital care, to pay; not file as "under observation" which is under Medicare Part B, outpatient care. Generally, your ER doctor will not follow your care, but turn it over to a hospitalist

The Part D "Donut Hole" is going away? This is a fact… but the Affordable Care Act or Obamacare is slowly closing the "Donut Hole" between now and the year 2020. Don't know why it is taking so long!! I have noticed that costs of drugs are escalating causing many to go in the donut hole faster. I advise everyone to do prescription drug planning to avoid the donut hole.

Toni Says® Many retirees are losing retiree benefits and the companies are using Medicare Advantage plans as an option. Always check with your doctor when this happens. Email us at **info@tonisays.com** for your specific situation.

Fact 8: Doctor's New Rule… Pay Up Front and YOU… File with Medicare!

Hi Toni

I have Original Medicare and a Medicare Supplement Plan F. No problem in the past filing with Medicare, but beginning January 1st, my neurologist has changed how he bills Medicare. He is a small office and said that because of the amount of paperwork, he is no longer filing with Medicare

I would have to pay up front and be reimbursed by Medicare. Can you please tell me what I need to do to submit this visit for reimbursement? Could this be the beginning of doctor problems because of Obamacare?

Thank you so much –Susan … Dallas, Texas

Hello Susan

This year's Medicare's open enrollment has a completely different "environment" because many of the Medicare beneficiaries are concerned they are going to lose their doctors if they have Original Medicare with a supplement or many that are members of a Medicare Advantage plan were informed that their doctors or specialists were no longer part of that specific Medicare Advantage plan.

People really do not like change, especially when it comes to their healthcare and the doctor, who they have faith in.

In these trying economic times that we are in and with all of the changes with Medicare, as you are experiencing, many doctors are not accepting Medicare and will not bill Medicare for you. They want you to submit the bill to Medicare and wait to be reimbursed.

Does your neurologist or any specialist charge Medicare rates or did the doctor's office charge you their rates and want you to be reimbursed from Medicare what Medicare rate will be? That is what it sounds like to me. And who knows how long it takes for Medicare to reimburse you.

Here are a few tips that I tell my clients which can help you when having this problem:

Before you set the appointment ask the doctor's office if they accept **Medicare assignment** and will bill Medicare directly for you. (This will be your easiest way.)

b. If they say **NO,** then you need to decide. Do I want to pay out of pocket and get reimbursed what Medicare pays? Doctors know they are not paid their asking rates. Medicare is not the only one who discounts the doctor's bills. Group health insurance also discounts the doctor's bills… OR…

Look for a doctor or specialist that does take **Medicare assignment** and will bill Medicare. There are still plenty of fantastic doctors/specialist that do accept Medicare. More doctors and specialists are taking Medicare than those that don't. Ask your primary care doctor/ specialist for more than one doctor or specialist that he/she can refer for you.

Toni's Tip: on how to file a Medicare claim

Here is how to file a claim if your doctor doesn't accept Medicare assignment. You may have to pay the complete bill and submit the claim to Medicare. See "What is assignment?" in the Medicare and You Handbook it explains how to submit a claim if your doctor, provider or supplier doesn't accept assignment. You can call 1/800-MEDICARE (633-4227) and ask for Form CMS-1490S or go to www.medicare.gov/ medicareonlineforms

While you have Medicare on the phone, ask them for help with filing the claim and they will be happy to assist.

Fact 9: Do Veterans Using the VA Qualify for Medicare??

Dear Toni

I am a Viet Nam Vet, turning 65 this May and recently, I was at the VA when someone told me that if I use the VA for my Medicare benefits that I cannot enroll in Medicare

I shed blood for my VA benefits and don't want to lose them because I enroll in Medicare. My wife reads your column and informs me that I will get a penalty if I enroll later. I really do not know what to do. I don't want to lose my VA benefit. What am I going to do?

Leroy from Lufkin, TX

Thanks Leroy,

I am glad hear that your wife reads my column because she has saved you tons of Medicare stress. Enrolling in original Medicare which is Parts A and B will not cause you to lose your VA medical benefits. In fact, enrolling in Medicare helps you if you need medical benefits outside of the VA

For someone to qualify for Medicare you must work and paid Social Security and Medicare taxes from your payroll check? Each individual has to work 10 years or 40 quarters to qualify for Medicare Part A at no cost. You have to enroll in Part B which has a monthly premium (the Medicare Part B premium is subject to change each year).

I would advise you and any Veteran reading this article to enroll in Medicare Parts A and B. In fact, the VA encourages Veterans to enroll in Part B.

I am very well aware that you do not need "Part B" to receive medical care from the VA, but when you go outside of the VA, for any medical treatment you do need Part B. You might be ambulanced to another hospital that is not a VA facility for a medical emergency, or you may go to MD Anderson for cancer treatment as examples, then you will pay 100% of the medical charges that "Part B" covers because you do not have Part B.

Part B covers all of your outpatient needs, doctor services such as office visits and even surgery, MRIs, chemotherapy and the list can go on. Without Part B of Medicare, a person might have to pay

100% out their pocket for services associated with Part B and this could be in the $1,000s or hundreds of thousands of dollars

Chemotherapy is usually done on an outpatient basis which falls under Medicare Part B. I don't know how much chemotherapy is, but if you are not enrolled in Part B, then you will pay 100% for the chemo if it is not received at the VA. I wouldn't want you to take that chance

Many who do not enroll in Part B when they are first eligible for Medicare, may have to pay a "late enrollment" penalty of 10% for each full 12-month period that you could have had Part B, but did not sign up for it

Let's says you waited 50 months, which is a 4 full 12-month period, then the Part B penalty is an additional 40% added to the current Part B premium for as long as you have Medicare.

But not enrolling in Part D (Medicare Prescription Drug plan) is another story. Medicare considers the VA credible coverage and when you enroll in Part D at a later date, you do not get the late enrollment penalty. Guess what, using the VA pharmacy you will have no Part D donut hole!

Thank You for your sacrifice and as my Husband always says, "Welcome Home"

Toni Says® If you are a Veteran…enroll in Part B when you either turn 65 or are coming off your company benefits. Medicare Part B is more valuable than you can imagine.

Fact 10: Moving Overseas…Should I Keep My Medicare?

Hello, Toni:

My husband and I are currently on Medicare with Part B, a supplement, and Part D coverage. We will be moving overseas for a couple of years. I know that there is no coverage from Medicare for overseas expenses

Is there a way to suspend our Medicare coverage (and the supplements & Part D) while we are overseas and reinstate it without a penalty when we return? It's a large expense to have to pay premiums in both countries, but only to have benefit from one. If we were to drop the supplement and Part D while we are gone, would we have to be underwritten if we return (i.e. excluded if we have pre-existing conditions)?

Thanks for your help with this. Part of our planning is trying to figure out our expenses while we are out of the country

Thank You…Sandy, Houston, TX

Good day, Sandy:

That's a great question. Will you or your husband be working full time with true company benefits? Or are you just moving out of the country for a few years to get away?

If you or your husband will be working with company benefits, then you can delay Part B until you return to the States without getting the "famous" Medicare Part B penalty.

If not working full-time with company benefits, then I would advise you and your husband to remain enrolled in Medicare and keep your Medicare Supplemental/Medigap plan because no one ever knows what will happen to your health in the future.

If you decide to drop your Medicare Supplement/Medigap and return to the United States later, you will be subject to underwriting and have to answer health questions to re-enroll into a new Medicare Supplement/Medigap for both you and your husband.

Yours is not the first question that I have received about stopping one's Medicare Part B when moving overseas and then one has a serious health issue. You then want to return to the US and re-enroll in Medicare Part B only to discover that your Medicare Part B penalty will go all the way back to the day you turned 65 at a 10% penalty for each year to when you were 65.

Let's say you and your spouse are 75 years old when you return to the States and re-enroll in Medicare. Your and your spouse's Medicare Part B penalty will be 75 - 65 = 10 years times 10% or 100% penalty. Not for one month, but for the rest of your and your spouse's Medicare enrollment

Not only will you have a Medicare penalty, but you will also have a Medicare Part D penalty because you let your Part D prescription drug plan expire. The only way to keep from having a Part D penalty is to have been enrolled in any type of creditable prescription drug coverage such as company benefits or VA prescription drug plan.

Toni Says® When you either do not enroll in Medicare Part B or you decide to cancel your Part B because you are moving out of the country and want to reenroll at a later date, you will have thefamous Part B penalty which will go back to the day you turned 65. Remember Medicare does not haveany do-over rules.

Fact 11: Medicare Annual Enrollment Tips

Below are a few tips to simplify your Medicare Annual Enrollment or if you are new to Medicare and want to make the best choice you can:

Medicare Tip #1: Know what Original Medicare covers…and what it doesn't. What your Part A deductible is and for Part B that Medicare pays 80% of approved charges while you pay 20% and a once a year deductible with a monthly premium that depends on your income. Plans like Medicare Supplement and Medicare Advantage help to cover the 20% gap with some offering extra benefits like vision, dental, hearing or fitness memberships. *Resources you may be interested n:* **http://tonisays.com**

Medicare Tip #2: Learn your Medicare ABC and Ds. Part A is hospital coverage. Part B is for medical/outpatient coverage such as doctor visits and performing surgery. Part C is Medicare Advantage plans that combine both Part A and B benefits with some plans having Part D included. Part D is for prescription drugs with the "famous" donut hole and can be in Part C or a standalone plan.

Medicare Tip #3: Keep in mind not all Medicare plans are created equal Plans and benefits differ from company to company and even state to state. Do your research especially is you will be moving to a new area.

Medicare Tip #4 Research Medicare Part D plans every Medicare Annual Enrollment Plans can change benefits and the drug formulary for the next year.

Medicare Tip #5: Don't choose on premium alone. Make sure there aren't hidden copays or other fees that will end up costing you more money.

Chapter 8
Forms

1. Request for Employment Information-CMS L-564
2. Application for Enrollment in Medicare Part B (Medical Insurance) CMS-40B
3. Medicare Income-Related Monthly Adjustment Amount – Life-Changing Event SSA-44 (OMB No. 0960-0784)
4. Medicare Easy Pay
5. What You Can Do Online
6. Medicare Costs

Form Approved
OMB No. 0938-0787
Expires: 06/2023

REQUEST FOR EMPLOYMENT INFORMATION

WHAT IS THE PURPOSE OF THIS FORM?

In order to apply for Medicare in a Special Enrollment Period, you must have or had group health plan coverage within the last 8 months through your or your spouse's current employment. People with disabilities must have large group health plan coverage based on your, your spouse's or a family member's current employment.

This form is used for proof of group health care coverage based on current employment. This information is needed to process your Medicare enrollment application.

The employer that provides the group health plan coverage completes the information about your health care coverage and dates of employment.

HOW IS THE FORM COMPLETED?

- Complete the first section of the form so that the employer can find and complete the information about your coverage and the employment of the person through which you have that health coverage.
- The employer fills in the information in the second section and signs at the bottom.

WHAT DO I DO WITH THE FORM?

Fill out Section A and take the form to your employer. Ask your employer to fill out Section B. You need to get the completed form from your employer and include it with your Application for Enrollment in Medicare (CMS-40B). Then you send both together to your local Social Security office. Find your local office here: **www.ssa.gov**.

GET HELP WITH THIS FORM

- **Phone:** Call Social Security at **1-800-772-1213**
- **En español:** Llame a SSA gratis al **1-800-772-1213** y oprima el 2 si desea el servicio en español y espere a que le atienda un agente.
- **In person:** Your local Social Security office. For an office near you check **www.ssa.gov**.

You have the right to get Medicare information in an accessible format, like large print, Braille, or audio. You also have the right to file a complaint if you feel you've been discriminated against. Visit https://www.medicare.gov/about-us/accessibility-nondiscrimination-notice, or call 1-800-MEDICARE (1-800-633-4227) for more information. TTY users can call 1-877-486-2048.

Form Approved
OMB No. 0938-0787

REQUEST FOR EMPLOYMENT INFORMATION

SECTION A: To be completed by individual signing up for Medicare Part B (Medical Insurance)

1. Employer's Name

2. Date __ __ / __ __ / __ __ __ __

3. Employer's Address

City

State

Zip Code

4. Applicant's Name

5. Applicant's Social Security Number __ __ __ – __ __ – __ __ __ __

6. Employee's Name

7. Employee's Social Security Number __ __ __ – __ __ – __ __ __ __

SECTION B: To be completed by Employers

For Employer Group Health Plans ONLY:

1. Is (or was) the applicant covered under an employer group health plan? ☐ Yes ☐ No

2. If yes, give the date the applicant's coverage began. (mm/yyyy)
__ __ / __ __ __ __

3. Has the coverage ended? ☐ Yes ☐ No

4. If yes, give the date the coverage ended. (mm/yyyy)
__ __ / __ __ __ __

5. When did the employee work for your company?
From: (mm/yyyy) __ __ / __ __ __ __
To: (mm/yyyy) __ __ / __ __ __ __
Still Employed: (mm/yyyy) __ __ / __ __ __ __

6. If you're a large group health plan and the applicant is disabled, please list the timeframe (all months) that your group health plan was primary payer.
From: (mm/yyyy) __ __ / __ __ __ __
To: (mm/yyyy) __ __ / __ __ __ __

For Hours Bank Arrangements ONLY:

1. Is (or was) the applicant covered under an Hours Bank Arrangement? ☐ Yes ☐ No

2. If yes, does the applicant have hours remaining in reserve? ☐ Yes ☐ No

3. Date reserve hours ended or will be used? (mm/yyyy)
__ __ / __ __ __ __

All Employers:

Signature of Company Official

Date Signed __ __ / __ __ / __ __ __ __

Title of Company Official

Phone Number (__ __ __) __ __ __ – __ __ __ __

Form Approved
OMB No. 0938-1230
Expires: 04/24

APPLICATION FOR ENROLLMENT IN MEDICARE PART B (MEDICAL INSURANCE)

WHO CAN USE THIS APPLICATION?

People with Medicare who have Part A but not Part B

NOTE: If you do **not** have Part A, do **not** complete this form. Contact Social Security if you want to apply for Medicare for the first time.

WHEN DO YOU USE THIS APPLICATION?

Use this form:

- If you're in your **Initial Enrollment Period** (IEP) and live in **Puerto Rico**. You must sign up for Part B using this form.
- If you're in your **IEP** and **refused Part B** or did not sign up when you applied for Medicare, but now want Part B.
- If you want to sign up for Part B during the General Enrollment Period (GEP) from January 1 – March 31 each year.
- If you refused Part B during your IEP because you had group health plan (GHP) coverage through your or your spouse's current employment. You may sign up during your 8-month Special Enrollment Period (SEP).
- If you have Medicare due to disability and refused Part B during your IEP because you had group health plan coverage through your, your spouse or family member's current employment.
- You may sign up during your 8-month SEP.

NOTE: Your IEP lasts for 7 months. It begins 3 months before your 65th birthday (or 25th month of disability) and ends 3 months after you reach 65 (or 3 months after the 25th month of disability).

WHAT INFORMATION DO YOU NEED TO COMPLETE THIS APPLICATION?

You will need:

- Your Medicare Number
- Your current address and phone number
- Form CMS-L564 "Request for Employment Information" completed by your employer **if you're signing up in a SEP**.

WHAT HAPPENS NEXT?

Send your completed and signed application to your local Social Security office. If you sign up in a SEP, include the CMS-L564 with your Part B application. If you have questions, call Social Security at **1-800-772-1213. TTY users should call 1-800-325-0778.**

HOW DO YOU GET HELP WITH THIS APPLICATION?

- **Phone:** Call Social Security at **1-800-772-1213**. **TTY users should call 1-800-325-0778.**
- **En español:** Llame a SSA gratis al **1-800-772-1213** y oprima el 2 si desea el servicio en español y espere a que le atienda un agente.
- **In person:** Your local Social Security office. For an office near you check www.ssa.gov.

REMINDERS

- If you sign up for Part B, you must pay premiums for every month you have the coverage.
- If you sign up after your IEP, you may have to pay a late enrollment penalty (LEP) of 10% for each full 12-month period you don't have Part B but were eligible to sign up.

You have the right to get Medicare information in an accessible format, like large print, Braille, or audio. You also have the right to file a complaint if you feel you've been discriminated against. Visit https://www.medicare.gov/about-us/accessibility-nondiscrimination-notice, or call 1-800-MEDICARE (1-800-633-4227) for more information. TTY users can call 1-877-486-2048.

Form Approved
OMB No. 0938-1230
Expires: 04/24

APPLICATION FOR ENROLLMENT IN MEDICARE PART B (MEDICAL INSURANCE)

1. Your Medicare Number

2. Do you wish to sign up for Medicare Part B (Medical Insurance)? ☐ YES

3. Your Name (Last Name, First Name, Middle Name)

4. Mailing Address (Number and Street, P.O. Box, or Route)

5. City State Zip Code

6. Phone Number (including area code)

( ) –

7. Written Signature (DO NOT PRINT)

SIGN HERE

8. Date Signed

/ /

IF THIS APPLICATION HAS BEEN SIGNED BY MARK (X), A WITNESS WHO KNOWS THE APPLICANT MUST SUPPLY THE INFORMATION REQUESTED BELOW.

9. Signature of Witness

10. Date Signed

/ /

11. Address of Witness

12. Remarks

According to the Paperwork Reduction Act of 1995, no persons are required to respond to a collection of information unless it displays a valid OMB control number. The valid OMB control number for this information collection is 0938-1230. The time required to complete this information is estimated to average 15 minutes per response, including the time to review instructions, search existing data resources, gather the data needed, and complete and review the information collection. If you have any comments concerning the accuracy of the time estimate(s) or suggestions for improving this form, please write to: CMS, Attn: PRA Reports Clearance Officer, 7500 Security Boulevard, Baltimore, Maryland 21244-1850.

SPECIAL MESSAGE FOR INDIVIDUAL APPLYING FOR PART B

This form is your application for Medicare Part B (Medical Insurance). You can use this form to sign up for Part B:

- During your Initial Enrollment Period (IEP) when you're first eligible for Medicare
- During the General Enrollment Period (GEP) from January 1 through March 31 of each year
- If you're eligible for a Special Enrollment Period (SEP), like if you're covered under a group health plan (GHP) based on current employment.

Initial Enrollment Period

Your IEP is the first chance you have to sign up for Part B. It lasts for 7 months. It begins 3 months before the month you reach 65, and it ends 3 months after you reach 65. If you have Medicare due to disability, your IEP begins 3 months before the 25th month of getting Social Security Disability benefits, and it ends 3 months after the 25th month of getting Social Security Disability benefits. To have Part B coverage start the month you're 65 (or the 25th month of disability insurance benefits); you must sign up in the first 3 months of your IEP. If you sign up in any of the remaining 4 months, your Part B coverage will start later.

General Enrollment Period

If you don't sign up for Part B during your IEP, you can sign up during the GEP. The GEP runs from January 1 through March 31 of each year. If you sign up during a GEP, your Part B coverage begins July 1 of that year. You may have to pay a late enrollment penalty if you sign up during the GEP. The cost of your Part B premium will go up 10% for each 12-month period that you could have had Part B but didn't sign up. You may have to pay this late enrollment penalty as long as you have Part B coverage.

Special Enrollment Period

If you don't sign up for Part B during your IEP, you can sign up without a late enrollment penalty during a Special Enrollment Period (SEP). If you think that you may be eligible for a SEP, please contact Social Security at 1-800-772-1213. TTY users should call 1-800-325-0778 You can use a SEP when your IEP has ended. The most common SEPs apply to the working aged, disabled, and international volunteers.

Working Aged/Disabled

You have a SEP if you're covered under a group health plan (GHP) based on ***current*** employment. To use this SEP, you must:

- Be 65 or older and currently employed
- Be the spouse of an employed person, and covered under your spouse's employer GHP based on his/her current employment
- Be under 65 and disabled, and covered under a GHP based on your own or your spouse's current employment

You can sign up for Part B anytime while you have a GHP coverage based on current employment or during the 8 months after either the coverage ends or the employment ends, whichever happens first. If you sign up while you have GHP coverage based on current employment, or, during the first full month that you no longer have this coverage, your Part B coverage will begin the first day of the month you sign up. You can also choose to have your coverage begin with any of the following 3 months. If you sign up during any of the remaining 7 months of your SEP, your Part B coverage will begin the month after you sign up.

NOTE: COBRA coverage or a retiree health plan is not considered group health plan coverage based on current employment.

International Volunteers

You have a SEP if you were volunteering outside of the United States for at least 12 months for a tax-exempt organization and had health insurance (through the organization) that provided coverage for the duration of the volunteer service.

PRIVACY ACT STATEMENT: Social Security is authorized to collect your information under sections 1836, 1840, and 1872 of the Social Security Act, as amended (42 U.S.C. 1395o, 1395s, and 1395ii) for your enrollment in Medicare Part B. Social Security and the Centers for Medicare & Medicaid Services (CMS) need your information to determine if you're entitled to Part B. While you don't have to give your information, failure to give all or part of the information requested on this form could delay your application for enrollment.
Social Security and CMS will use your information to enroll you in Part B. Your information may be also be used to administer Social Security or CMS programs or other programs that coordinate with Social Security or CMS to:
1)Determine your rights to Social Security benefits and/or Medicare coverage.
2)Comply with Federal laws requiring Social Security and CMS records (like to the Government Accountability Office and the VeteransAdministration)
3)Assist with research and audit activities necessary to protect integrity and improve Social Security and CMS programs (like to the Bureau ofthe Census and contractors of Social Security and CMS).We may verify your information using computer matches that help administer Social Security and CMS programs in accordance with theComputer Matching and Privacy Protection Act of 1988 (P.L. 100-503).

STEP BY STEP INSTRUCTIONS FOR FILLING OUT THIS APPLICATION

1. **Your Medicare Number:**
   Write your Medicare number.

2. **Do you wish to sign up for Medicare Part B (Medical Insurance)?**
   Mark "YES" in this field if you want to sign up for Medicare Part B which provides you with medical insurance under Medicare. You can only sign up using this form if you already have Medicare Part A (Hospital Insurance). If your answer to this question is "no" then you don't need to fill out this application. This application is to sign up to get medical insurance under Medicare.

   If you don't have Part A and want to sign up, please contact Social Security at 1-800-772-1213. TTY users should call 1-800-325-0778.

3. **Name:**
   Write your name as you did when you applied for Social Security or Medicare. List last name, first name and middle name in that order. If you don't have a middle name, leave it blank.

4. **Mailing Address:**
   Write your full mailing address including the number and street name, P.O. Box, or route in this field.

5. **City, State, and ZIP code:**
   Write the city name, state and ZIP code for the mailing address.

6. **Phone Number:**
   Write your 10-digit phone number, including area code.

7. **Written Signature:**
   Sign your name in this section in the same way you would sign it for any other official document. Do not print.

   If you're unable to sign, you may mark an "X" in this field. In this case, you will need a witness and the witness must complete questions 11, 12 and 13.

8. **Date Signed:**
   Write the date that you signed the application.

9. **Signature of Witness:**
   In the case that question 9 is signed by an "X" instead of a written signature, a witness signature is needed in question 11 showing that the person who signs the application is the person represented on the application.

10. **Date Signed:**
    If a witness signs this application, the witness must provide the date of the signature.

11. **Address of Witness:**
    If a witness signs this application, provide the witness's address.

12. **Remarks:**
    Provide any remarks or comments on the form to clarify information about your enrollment application.

IMPORTANT INFORMATION:

Review the scenario below to determine if you need to include additional information or forms with your application.

If you're signing up for Part B using a Special Enrollment Period (SEP) because you were covered under a group health plan based on current employment, in addition to this application, you will also need to have your employer fill out and return the "Request for Employment Information" form (**CMS-L564/CMS-R-297**) with your application. The purpose of this form is to provide documentation to Social Security that proves that you have been continuously covered by a group health plan based on current employment, with no more than 8 consecutive months of not having coverage. If your employer went out of business or refuses to complete the form, please contact Social Security about other information you may be able to provide to process your SEP enrollment request.

Send the application (and the "Request for Employment Information," if applicable) to your local Social Security Office. Find your local office at **www.ssa.gov**.

Medicare Income-Related Monthly Adjustment Amount - Life-Changing Event

If you had a major life-changing event and your income has gone down, you may use this form to request a reduction in your income-related monthly adjustment amount. See page 5 for detailed information and line-by-line instructions. If you prefer to schedule an interview with your local Social Security office, call 1-800-772-1213 (TTY 1-800-325-0778).

Name	**Social Security Number**

You may use this form if you received a notice that your monthly Medicare Part B (medical insurance) or prescription drug coverage premiums include an income-related monthly adjustment amount (IRMAA) and you experienced a life-changing event that may reduce your IRMAA. To decide your IRMAA, we asked the Internal Revenue Service (IRS) about your adjusted gross income plus certain tax-exempt income which we call "modified adjusted gross income" or MAGI from the Federal income tax return you filed for tax year 2019. If that was not available, we asked for your tax return information for 2018. We took this information and used the table below to decide your income-related monthly adjustment amount.

The table below shows the income-related monthly adjustment amounts for Medicare premiums based on your tax filing status and income. If your MAGI was lower than $91,000.01 (or lower than $182,000.01 if you filed your taxes with the filing status of married, filing jointly) in your most recent filed tax return, you do not have to pay any income-related monthly adjustment amount. If you do not have to pay an income-related monthly adjustment amount, you should not fill out this form even if you experienced a life-changing event.

If you filed your taxes as:	***And your MAGI was:***	***Your Part B monthly adjustment is:***	***Your prescription drug coverage monthly adjustment is:***
-Single, -Head of household, -Qualifying widow(er) with dependent child, or -Married filing separately (and you did not live with your spouse in tax year)*	$ 91,000.01 - $114,000.00 $114,000.01 - $142,000.00 $142,000.01 - $170,000.00 $170,000.01 - $499,999.99 More than $499,999.99	$ 68.00 $170.10 $272.20 $374.20 $408.20	$ 12.40 $ 32.10 $ 51.70 $ 71.30 $ 77.90
-Married, filing jointly	$182,000.01 - $228,000.00 $228,000.01 - $284,000.00 $284,000.01 - $340,000.00 $340,000.01 - $749,999.99 More than $750,000.00	$ 68.00 $170.10 $272.20 $374.20 $408.20	$ 12.40 $ 32.10 $ 51.70 $ 71.30 $ 77.90
-Married, filing separately (and you lived with your spouse during part of that tax year)*	$91,000.01 - $408,999.99 More than $409,000.00	$374.20 $408.20	$ 71.30 $ 77.90

* Let us know if your tax filing status for the tax year was Married, filing separately, but you lived apart from your spouse at all times during that tax year.

STEP 1: Type of Life-Changing Event

Check **ONE** life-changing event and fill in the date that the event occurred (mm/dd/yyyy). If you had more than one life-changing event, please call Social Security at 1-800-772-1213 (TTY 1-800-325-0778).

- ☐ Marriage
- ☐ Divorce/Annulment
- ☐ Death of Your Spouse
- ☐ Work Stoppage
- ☐ Work Reduction
- ☐ Loss of Income-Producing Property
- ☐ Loss of Pension Income
- ☐ Employer Settlement Payment

Date of life-changing event: ______________
mm/dd/yyyy

STEP 2: Reduction in Income

Fill in the tax year in which your income was reduced by the life-changing event (see instructions on page 6), the amount of your adjusted gross income (AGI, as used on line 11 of IRS form 1040) and tax-exempt interest income (as used on line 2a of IRS form 1040), and your tax filing status.

Tax Year	Adjusted Gross Income	Tax-Exempt Interest
20__ __	$ __ __ __ __ __ __ . __ __	$ __ __ __ __ __ __ . __ __

Tax Filing Status for this Tax Year (choose **ONE**):

- ☐ Single
- ☐ Head of Household
- ☐ Qualifying Widow(er) with Dependent Child
- ☐ Married, Filing Jointly
- ☐ Married, Filing Separately

STEP 3: Modified Adjusted Gross Income

Will your modified adjusted gross income be lower next year than the year in Step 2?

- ☐ No - Skip to STEP 4
- ☐ Yes - Complete the blocks below for next year

Tax Year	Estimated Adjusted Gross Income	Estimated Tax-Exempt Interest
20__ __	$ __ __ __ __ __ __ . __ __	$ __ __ __ __ __ __ . __ __

Expected Tax Filing Status for this Tax Year (choose **ONE**):

- ☐ Single
- ☐ Head of Household
- ☐ Qualifying Widow(er) with Dependent Child
- ☐ Married, Filing Jointly
- ☐ Married, Filing Separately

STEP 4: Documentation

Provide evidence of your modified adjusted gross income (MAGI) and your life-changing event. You can either:

1. Attach the required evidence and we will mail your original documents or certified copies back to you;

OR

2. Show your original documents or certified copies of evidence of your life-changing event and modified adjusted gross income to an SSA employee.

Note: You must sign in Step 5 and attach all required evidence. Make sure that you provide your current address and a phone number so that we can contact you if we have any questions about your request.

STEP 5: Signature

PLEASE READ THE FOLLOWING INFORMATION CAREFULLY BEFORE SIGNING THIS FORM.

I understand that the Social Security Administration (SSA) will check my statements with records from the Internal Revenue Service to make sure the determination is correct.

I declare under penalty of perjury that I have examined the information on this form and it is true and correct to the best of my knowledge.

I understand that signing this form does not constitute a request for SSA to use more recent tax year information unless it is accompanied by:

- **Evidence that I have had the life-changing event indicated on this form;**
- **A copy of my Federal tax return; or**
- **Other evidence of the more recent tax year's modified adjusted gross income.**

Signature	**Phone Number**	
Mailing Address	**Apartment Number**	
City	**State**	**ZIP Code**

THE PRIVACY ACT

We are required by sections 1839(i) and 1860D-13 of the Social Security Act to ask you to give us the information on this form. This information is needed to determine if you qualify for a reduction in your monthly Medicare Part B and/or prescription drug coverage income-related monthly adjustment amount (IRMAA). In order for us to determine if you qualify, we need to evaluate information that you provide to us about your modified adjusted gross income. Although the responses are voluntary, if you do not provide the requested information we will not be able to consider a reduction in your IRMAA.

We rarely use the information you supply for any purpose other than for determining a potential reduction in IRMAA. However, the law sometimes requires us to give out the facts on this form without your consent. We may release this information to another Federal, State, or local government agency to assist us in determining your eligibility for a reduction in your IRMAA, if Federal law requires that we do so, or to do the research and audits needed to administer or improve our efforts for the Medicare program.

We may also use the information you provide in computer matching programs. Matching programs compare our records with records kept by other Federal, state or local government agencies. We will also compare the information you give us to your tax return records maintained by the IRS. The law allows us to do this even if you do not agree to it. Information from these matching programs can be used to establish or verify a person's eligibility for Federally funded or administered benefit programs and for repayment of payments or delinquent debts under these programs.

Explanations about these and other reasons why information you provide us may be used or given out are available in Systems of Records Notice 60-0321 (Medicare Database File). The Notice, additional information about this form, and any other information regarding our systems and programs, are available on-line at www.socialsecurity.gov or at your local Social Security office.

Paperwork Reduction Act Statement - This information collection meets the requirements of 44 U.S.C. § 3507, as amended by section 2 of the Paperwork Reduction Act of 1995. You do not need to answer these questions unless we display a valid Office of Management and Budget control number. We estimate that it will take about 45 minutes to read the instructions, gather the facts, and answer the questions. **SEND OR BRING THE COMPLETED FORM TO YOUR LOCAL SOCIAL SECURITY OFFICE. The office is listed under U. S. Government agencies in your telephone directory or you may call Social Security at 1-800-772-1213 (TTY 1-800-325-0778).** *You may send comments on our time estimate above to: SSA, 6401 Security Blvd, Baltimore, MD 21235-6401.* ***Send only comments relating to our time estimate to this address, not the completed form.***

INSTRUCTIONS FOR COMPLETING FORM SSA-44
Medicare Income-Related Monthly Adjustment Amount
Life-Changing Event--Request for Use of More Recent Tax Year Information

You do not have to complete this form in order to ask that we use your information about your modified adjusted gross income for a more recent tax year. If you prefer, you may call 1-800-772-1213 and speak to a representative from 7 a.m. until 7 p.m. on business days to request an appointment at one of our field offices. If you are hearing-impaired, you may call our TTY number, 1-800-325-0778.

Identifying Information

Print your full name and your own Social Security Number as they appear on your Social Security card. Your Social Security Number may be different from the number on your Medicare card.

STEP 1

You should choose only one life-changing event on the list. If you experienced more than one life-changing event, please call your local Social Security office at 1-800-772-1213 (TTY 1-800-325-0778). Fill in the date that the life-changing event occurred. The life-changing event date must be in the same year or an earlier year than the tax year you ask us to use to decide your income-related premium adjustment. For example, if we used your 2018 tax information to determine your income-related monthly adjustment amount for 2020, you can request that we use your 2019 tax information instead if you experienced a reduction in your income in 2018 due to a life-changing event that occurred in 2019 or an earlier year.

Life-Changing Event	Use this category if...
Marriage	You entered into a legal marriage.
Divorce/Annulment	Your legal marriage ended, and you will not file a joint return with your spouse for the year.
Death of Your Spouse	Your spouse died.
Work Stoppage or Reduction	You or your spouse stopped working or reduced the hours that you work.
Loss of Income-Producing Property	You or your spouse experienced a loss of income-producing property that was not at your direction (e.g., not due to the sale or transfer of the property). This includes loss of real property in a Presidentially or Gubernatorially-declared disaster area, destruction of livestock or crops due to natural disaster or disease, or loss of property due to arson, or loss of investment property due to fraud or theft.
Loss of Pension Income	You or your spouse experienced a scheduled cessation, termination, or reorganization of an employer's pension plan.
Employer Settlement Payment	You or your spouse receive a settlement from an employer or former employer because of the employer's bankruptcy or reorganization.

INSTRUCTIONS FOR COMPLETING FORM SSA-44

STEP 2

Supply information about the more recent year's modified adjusted gross income (MAGI). Note that this year must reflect a reduction in your income due to the life-changing event you listed in Step 1. A change in your tax filing status due to the life-changing event might also reduce your income-related monthly adjustment amount. Your MAGI is your adjusted gross income as used on line 11 of IRS form 1040 plus your tax-exempt interest income as used on line 2a of IRS form 1040. We used your MAGI and your tax filing status to determine your income-related monthly adjustment amount.

Tax Year

- Fill in both empty spaces in the box that says "20_ _". The year you choose must be more recent than the year of the tax return information we used. The letter that we sent you tells you what tax year we used.

  - Choose this year (the "premium year") - if your modified adjusted gross income is lower this year than last year. For example, if you request that we adjust your income-related premium for 2021, use your estimate of your 2020 MAGI if:

    1. Your income was not reduced until 2022; or
    2. Your income was reduced in 2021, but will be lower in 2022.

  - Choose last year (the year before the "premium year," which is the year for which you want us to adjust your IRMAA) - if your MAGI is not lower this year than last year. For example, if you request that we adjust your 2022 income-related monthly adjustment amounts and your income was reduced in 2020 by a life-changing event AND will be no lower in 2022, use your tax information for 2021.

  - Exception: If we used IRS information about your MAGI 3 years before the premium year, you may ask us to use information from 2 years before the premium year. For example, if we used your income tax return for 2019 to decide your 2022 IRMAA, you can ask us to use your 2020 information.

- If you have any questions about what year you should use, you should call SSA.

Adjusted Gross Income

- Fill in your actual or estimated adjusted gross income for the year you wrote in the "tax year" box. Adjusted gross income is the amount on line 11 of IRS form 1040. If you are providing an estimate, your estimate should be what you expect to enter on your tax return for that year.

Tax-exempt Interest Income

- Fill in your actual or estimated tax-exempt interest income for the tax year you wrote in the "tax year" box. Tax-exempt interest income is the amount reported on line 2a of IRS form 1040. If you are providing an estimate, your estimate should be what you expect to enter on your tax return for that year.

Filing Status

- Check the box in front of your actual or expected tax filing status for the year you wrote in the "tax year" box.

INSTRUCTIONS FOR COMPLETING FORM SSA-44

STEP 3

Complete this step only if you expect that your MAGI for next year will be even lower and will reduce your IRMAA below what you told us in Step 2 using the table on page 1. We will record this information and use it next year to determine your Medicare income-related monthly adjustment amounts. If you do not complete Step 3, we will use the information from Step 2 next year to determine your income-related monthly adjustment amounts, unless one of the conditions described in "Important Facts" on page 8 occurs.

Tax Year

- Fill in both empty spaces in the box that says "20 _ _" with the year following the year you wrote in Step 2. For example, if you wrote "2022" in Step 2, then write "2023" in Step 3.

Adjusted Gross Income

- Fill in your estimated adjusted gross income for the year you wrote in the "tax year" box. Adjusted gross income is the amount you expect to enter on line 11 of IRS form 1040 when you file your tax return for that year.

Tax-exempt Interest Income

- Fill in your estimated tax-exempt interest income for the tax year you wrote in the "tax year" box. Tax-exempt interest income is the amount you expect to report on line 2a of IRS form 1040.

Filing Status

- Check the box in front of your expected tax filing status for the year you wrote in the "tax year" box.

STEP 4

Provide your required evidence of your MAGI and your life-changing event.

Modified Adjusted Gross Income Evidence

If you have filed your Federal income tax return for the year you wrote in Step 2, then you must provide us with your signed copy of your tax return or a transcript from IRS. If you provided an estimate in Step 2, you must show us a signed copy of your tax return when you file your Federal income tax return for that year.

Life-Changing Event Evidence

We must see original documents or certified copies of evidence that the life-changing event occurred. Required evidence is described on the next page. In some cases, we may be able to accept another type of evidence if you do not have a preferred document listed on the next page. Ask a Social Security representative to explain what documents can be accepted.

Life-Changing Event	Evidence
Marriage	An original marriage certificate; or a certified copy of a public record of marriage.
Divorce/Annulment	A certified copy of the decree of divorce or annulment.
Death of Your Spouse	A certified copy of a death certificate, certified copy of the public record of death, or a certified copy of a coroner's certificate.
Work Stoppage or Reduction	An original signed statement from your employer; copies of pay stubs; original or certified documents that show a transfer of your business. **Note:** In the absence of such proof, we will accept your signed statement, under penalty of perjury, on this form, that you partially or fully stopped working or accepted a job with reduced compensation.
Loss of Income-Producing Property	An original copy of an insurance company adjuster's statement of loss or a letter from a State or Federal government about the uncompensated loss. If the loss was due to investment fraud (theft), we also require proof of conviction for the theft, such as a court document citing theft or fraud relating to you or your spouse's loss.
Loss of Pension Income	A letter or statement from your pension fund administrator that explains the reduction or termination of your benefits.
Employer Settlement Payment	A letter from the employer stating the settlement terms of the bankruptcy court and how it affects you or your spouse.

STEP 5

Read the information above the signature line, and sign the form. Fill in your phone number and current mailing address. It is very important that we have this information so that we can contact you if we have any questions about your request.

Important Facts

- When we use your estimated MAGI information to make a decision about your income-related monthly adjustment amount, we will later check with the IRS to verify your report.
- If you provide an estimate of your MAGI rather than a copy of your Federal tax return, we will ask you to provide a copy of your tax return when you file your taxes.
- If your estimate of your MAGI changes, or you amend your tax return for that reason, you will need to contact us to update our records. If you do not contact us, we may have to make corrections later including retroactive assessments or refunds.
- We will use your estimate provided in Step 2 to make a decision about the amount of your income-related monthly adjustment amounts the following year until:
  - IRS sends us your tax return information for the year used in Step 2; or
  - You provide a signed copy of your filed Federal income tax return or amended Federal income tax return with a different amount; or
  - You provide an updated estimate.
- If we used information from IRS about a tax year when your filing status was Married filing separately, but you lived apart from your spouse at all times during that year, you should contact us at 1-800-772-1213 (TTY 1-800-325-0778) to explain that you lived apart from your spouse. Do not use this form to report this change.

DEPARTMENT OF HEALTH & HUMAN SERVICES
Centers for Medicare & Medicaid Services
7500 Security Boulevard
Baltimore, Maryland 21244-1850

Thank you for your interest in Medicare Easy Pay. By completing and returning the Authorization Agreement for Preauthorized Payments form (SF-5510), you're authorizing the Centers for Medicare & Medicaid Services (CMS), the Federal agency that runs Medicare, to deduct your monthly Medicare premium from your bank account. This notice tells you what happens once you complete and return the form.

What information do I need to put on the form?

The form asks for basic information about you and your bank (also called a financial institution). **Have your red, white, and blue Medicare card and a blank check from your bank account with you when you fill out the form.**

Here are a few tips to help you:

When the form asks for	Do this
Individual/Organization Name	Enter your name the way it looks on your Medicare card.
Your Agency Account Identification Number	Enter your Medicare number from your Medicare card.
Type of Payment	Enter "Medicare Premiums" (this field is prefilled on the form).
Nine-Digit Routing Number	Enter the number from the bottom left corner of your check.
Account Title	Enter the name of the account holder or the individual who has power of attorney.
Account Number	Enter the checking or savings account number (don't use spaces or symbols).

If you're using a checking account to pay your premiums, attach a voided check for your checking account.

Where do I send the completed form?

Centers for Medicare & Medicaid Services
Medicare Premium Collection Center
P.O. Box 979098
St. Louis, MO 63197-9000

What happens once I return this form?

We'll process your form once we get it. Sometimes this can take 6 to 8 weeks. If we can't process your form, we'll return the form to you with a letter explaining why.

CMS Product No. 11636
January 2013

Two things will happen each month after your request is processed:

1. You'll get a Notice of Medicare Premium Payment Due stating, "This is not a bill" to let you know that the premium will be deducted from your bank account.

2. We'll deduct your premium from your bank account (usually on the 20th of the month). It will appear on your bank statement as an "Automated Clearing House (ACH)" transaction.

We'll only try to deduct your premium once each month. If your bank rejects or returns your premium deduction, we'll send you a letter with instructions on how to make a direct payment to Medicare.

Do I need to do anything when my premium amounts change?
No, we will automatically deduct the new premium amount from your bank account.

What if I want to change bank accounts or stop Medicare Easy Pay?
Complete another Authorization Agreement for Preauthorized Payments form (SF- 5510), and indicate the type of change you want to make. Mail the completed form to the address above. You can get a new form at **www.medicare.gov** or by calling 1-800-MEDICARE.

PREVIOUS EDITION NOT USABLE 6-8000

CMS Product No. 11636
January 2013

AUTHORIZATION AGREEMENT FOR PREAUTHORIZED PAYMENTS	**OMB Control Number: 1530-0015** **Expiration Date: 6/30/2020**

(AGENCY NAME)

Paperwork Reduction Act/Privacy Act Statement

The information requested on this form is required under the Electronic Fund Transfer Act (15 USC § 1693 et seq.), 12 CFR 205, and 31 CFR 206 and 210, for the purpose of authorizing the Department of the Treasury to electronically collect payments from your account. The information will be used to match the records of the government agency with those of the financial institution to direct your payments to the point you authorize. No pre-authorized electronic fund transfer from your account may be transacted unless a signed authorization form is received. Furnishing this information is voluntary; however, failure to furnish this information may delay or prevent the electronic collection of a payment through the Automated Clearing House. You are not required to respond to a collection of information unless it displays a valid OMB control number. The valid OMB control number for this collection of information is 1530-0015. We estimate that it will take approximately 15 minutes to complete this form.

CHECK ONE ☐ START ☐ CHANGE ☐ STOP

INDIVIDUAL/COMPANY INFORMATION

INDIVIDUAL/ORGANIZATION NAME *(Please Print)*

STREET ADDRESS

CITY/STATE	ZIP CODE

AREA CODE	TELEPHONE NUMBER

YOUR AGENCY ACCOUNT IDENTIFICATION NUMBER	TYPE OF PAYMENT

I hereby authorize the initiation of the debit entries from my account listed below and the financial institution named below to debit such account. I understand I will be notified if the debit amount needs to be adjusted, either to be increased or decreased. I also understand that I have the right to stop automatic payment by notifying my financial institution in writing three days prior to the time my account is to be charged. I/we acknowledge that the origination of ACH transactions to my/our account must comply with U.S. law. This authorization is to remain in full force and effect until the agency listed above has received written notification from me in such time and in such manner as to afford the agency listed above and the financial institution listed below a reasonable opportunity to act upon it.

SIGNATURE ______________________ DATE ____________

FINANCIAL INSTITUTION INFORMATION

FINANCIAL INSTITUTION NAME

STREET ADDRESS

CITY/STATE	ZIP CODE

NINE-DIGIT ROUTING TRANSIT NUMBER ▶ ☐☐☐☐☐☐☐☐☐

ACCOUNT TITLE

ACCOUNT NUMBER ☐ **CHECKING** ☐ **SAVINGS**

SIGNATURE AND TITLE OF REPRESENTATIVE	AREA CODE/TELEPHONE NUMBER	DATE

DEPARTMENT OF THE TREASURY
AUTHORIZED FOR LOCAL REPRODUCTION

PREVIOUS EDITION NOT USABLE

STANDARD FORM 5510 (REV. 3/2017)
Prescribed by 12 CFR 205; 31 CFR 206 and 210; I TFM 6-8000

What You Can Do Online
www.socialsecurity.gov

Apply for benefits
You can apply for many different Social Security benefits at ***www.socialsecurity.gov/applyonline***. • Apply for Social Security retirement/spouse's benefits; • Apply for Social Security disability benefits (and Supplemental Security Income (SSI) if applying at the same time and you meet other criteria); • Apply for Medicare and Extra Help with Medicare prescription drug costs.

Estimate your future benefits	
Create a my Social Security account to: • Get your Social Security Statement; • Check your earnings record; and • See estimates of your potential benefit amounts.	***www.socialsecurity.gov/myaccount***
Get your retirement benefit estimate based on your earnings record and when you might retire.	***www.socialsecurity.gov/estimator***
Use our planners to help you better understand your Social Security protection as you plan for your financial future. Then choose a benefit calculator to find out your monthly benefit amounts.	***www.socialsecurity.gov/planners***

If you get benefits	
Create a my Social Security account and • Get proof of your benefits; • Check your benefit and payment information and your earnings record; • Change your address and phone number; • Start or change direct deposit; • Get a replacement SSA-1099/1042S for tax season; • Report your wages if you work and receive disability benefits; and • Request a replacement Medicare card.	***www.socialsecurity.gov/myaccount***

Other things you can do online	
• Check the status of your claim. • Request a replacement Social Security card online, as long as you live in one of the participating states or the District of Columbia, are not requesting a name change or any other change to your card, and you meet other requirements.	***www.socialsecurity.gov/myaccount***
If your application for disability benefits was denied recently for medical reasons, you can request an appeal online or continue working on an appeal you already started.	***www.socialsecurity.gov/benefits/disability/appeal.html***

Contacting Social Security

The most convenient way to contact us anytime, anywhere is to visit ***www.socialsecurity.gov*** where you can also take care of some business with an online my Social Security account.

Call us toll-free at **1-800-772-1213** or at **1-800-325-0778** (TTY) if you're deaf or hard of hearing. We can answer your calls from 7 a.m. to 7 p.m., week days. Or use our auto-mated services via telephone, 24 hours a day. We look forward to serving you.

Social Security Administration
Publication No. 05-10121 | ICN 444812 | Unit of Issue — HD (one hundred)
December 2017 (September 2017 edition may be used)
What You Can Do Online
Produced and published at U.S. taxpayer expense

Printed on recycled paper

2022 Medicare Costs - Part A

What you pay for the Original Medicare Plan in 2022
Part A Costs for Covered Services and Items

Blood	You pay all costs for the first 3 pints of blood you get as an inpatient, then 20% of the Medicare-approved amount for additional pints of blood (unless you or someone else donate to replace what's used).
Home Health Care	You Pay $0 for home health care services and 20% of the Medicare-approved amount for durable medical equipment.
Hospice Care	You pay a co-payment of up to $5 per prescription for outpatient prescription drugs and 5% of Medicare-approved amount for inpatient respite care (short-term care given by another caregiver, so the usual caregiver can rest). You may have to pay room and board if you get hospice care in a facility other than for short-term general inpatient care or respite care.
Hospital Stay	You pay $1,556 deductible and no coinsurance for days 1-60 each benefit period $389 per day for days 61-90 each benefit period $778 per "lifetime reserve day" after day 90 each benefit period (up to 60 days over your lifetime). All costs for each day after the lifetime reserve days. Inpatient mental health care in a psychiatric hospital limited to 190 days in a lifetime.
Skilled Nursing Facility Stay	You pay $0 for the first 20 days each benefit period. $194.50 per day for days 21-100 each benefit period. All costs for each day after day 100 in the benefit period.

Note: All Medicare Advantage Plans must cover these services. Costs vary by plan but may either higher or lower than those noted above. Check with your plan.

**These deductibles and copayments change each year.

2022 Medicare Costs - Part B

What you pay for the Original Medicare Plan in 2022
Part B Costs for Covered Services and Items

Blood	You pay all costs for the first 3 pints of blood you get as an inpatient, then 20% of the Medicare-approved amount for additional pints of blood (unless you or someone else donates to replace what is used).
Clinical Laboratory Services	You Pay $0 for Medicare-approved services. The Part B deductible applies.
Home Health Services	You pay $0 for Medicare-approved services you pay 20% of the Medicare-approved amount for durable medical equipment. The Part B deductible applies.
Medical and Other Services	You pay 20% of the Medicare-approved amount for most doctor services, (including most doctor services during a hospital inpatient stay) outpatient therapy*, most preventive services, and durable medical equipment. The Part B deductible applies.
Mental Health	You pay 20% for most outpatient mental health care. The Part B deductible applies.
Other Covered Services	You pay co-payment or coinsurance amounts. The Part B deductible applies
Outpatient Hospital Services	You pay a coinsurance or co-payment amount that varies by services. The Part B deductible applies.
Part B Deductible	You pay the first $233 once a year for Part B-covered services or items.

*In 2022, there may be limits on physical therapy, occupational therapy, and speech-language pathology services. If so, there may be exceptions to these limits.

Note: All Medicare Advantage Plans must cover these services. Costs vary by plan but may be either higher or lower than those noted above. Check with your plan.
**These deductible and co-payments change each year.

Your 2022 Monthly Premiums for Medicare

Part A (Hospital Insurance) Monthly Premium

Most people do not pay a Part A Premium because they paid Medicare taxes while they worked. It takes 10 years or 40 quarters of working and paying taxes to qualify for Medicare. Those who did not work or pay into Social Security System for 10 years will not have Medicare under their Social Security Number and should use their spouses' Social Security number to qualify (if spouse worked 10+ years). Remember 10 years of paying into Social Security System is required to receive Medicare Part A premium free.

You will pay up to $499 each month if you do not qualify for premium free Medicare Part A. If you paid Medicare taxes for 30-39 quarters the standard Part A premium is $274 each month. If you pay a late enrollment penalty, this amount is higher.

Part B (Medical Insurance) 2022 Monthly Premium

If your Yearly Income is File Individual Tax Return	If your Yearly Income is File Joint Tax Return	You Pay
$91,000 or below	$182,000 or below	$170.10
$91,000.01-$114,000	$182,000.01-$228,000	$238.10
$114,000.01-$142,000	$228,000.01-$284,000	$340.20
$142,000.01-$170,000	$284,000.01-$340,000	$442.30
$170,000.01-500,000	$340,000.01-750,000	$544.30
Above $500,000.01	Above 750,000.01	$578.30

**Part B premium changes each year. Social Security will notify you through your yearly "New Benefit Report" late in November or December of each year. For questions regarding Part B premium, call Social Security at 1/800-722-1213. TTY users should call 1/800-325-0778.

Your 2022 Monthly Premiums for Medicare

Part C (Medical Advantage Plan) and Part D (Medicare Prescription Drug)

If your Yearly Income is File Individual Tax Return	If your Yearly Income is File Joint Tax Return	You Pay
$91,000 or below	$182,000 or below	Your Plan Premium
$91,000.01-$114,000	$182,000.01-$228,000	$12.30 + Your Plan Premium
$114,00.01-$142,000	$228,000.01-$284,000	$32.80 + Your Plan Premium
$142,000.01-$170,000	$284,000.01-$340,000	$51.70 + Your Plan Premium
$170,000.01-500,000	$340,000.01-$750,000	$71.30 + Your Plan Premium
Above $500,000.01	Above 750,000.01	$77.90 + Your Plan Premium

The income-related monthly adjustment amount will be deducted from your monthly Social Security check, no matter how you usually pay your plan premium. If the amount is more than your check, you will get a bill from Medicare. The figure below is used to estimate the Part D late enrollment penalty.

Part D National Base Beneficiary Premium is $33.37
1% Penalty Calculation is $0.3337

Medicare Disclaimer

This book/guide is not associated, endorsed, or authorized by the Social Security Administration, the Department of Health and Human Services or the Centers for Medicare & Medicaid Services. This book/guide contains basic information about Medicare, services related to Medicare and services for people with Medicare. If you would like to find more information about the Federal Government's program, please visit the official U.S. Government's Site for people with Medicare located at www.medicare.gov.

In Closing

The most important point of this entire book is that there are many rules to Medicare. You must learn them or the rules will hurt your pocket book. Many on Medicare live on a fixed income and making one costly mistake turns their retirement years into a nightmare. They constantly worry about how they are going to get by!

My advice is for you to ask questions. If you don't like the answers, then you have someone in your corner that can help you. That is ME!!! Email me at **info@tonisays.com** and one of the Toni Says® Medicare consultants can help you with your Medicare questions.

Once you understand Medicare, NO ONE can take that knowledge away from YOU!!!

There are 3 things to remember!

1. Most important thing to remember is ENROLLING IN MEDICRE PART B the correct way to keep from receiving a Medicare Part B penalty. Not enrolling in Medicare Part B can cost you thousands of dollars. Leaving you with more stress that you cannot even imagine.
2. Do prescription drug planning when enrolling in Medicare the first time and then remember to do it again when Medicare Annual Enrollment Period (Open Enrollment) happens from October 5th to December 7th every year. There can be serious changes to a Medicare Part D prescription drug plans for the next year.
3. Always discuss what Medicare plan your Medicare provider or facilities are accepting, when you want to make a change to the Medicare plan you are currently using, whether Original/Traditional Medicare with a Supplement/Medigap or a Medicare Advantage Plan

When you get an answer that you deep down, just don't think is right, remember to contact the Toni Says office at **info@tonisays.com**. Let the Toni Says team guide you through the maze of Medicare

Once you understand the maze of Medicare, you can go out and help someone else understand how Medicare works

Remember that's the American way! *One person helps another person*

My main intention when writing my first book was to help the average American understand, Medicare in simple terms. Since writing in the local Houston, TX papers, changes have taken place regarding those on Medicare with or without company benefits and retirees that are losing their retirement benefits they worked so hard for. What started as a guide to help Americans understand Medicare has turned into a mission. With God's help, I will keep helping Americans understand the maze of Medicare

Thank You and Many Blessings,

Toni

Bibliography

Medicare & You, 2019 edition, Baltimore, MD, September 2018

About Medicare, Retrieved on January 24, 2017. http://www.mymedicarematters.com

United States Government (September 2007).

SSA Publication No. 05-10043, Retrieved on January 24, 2017.

http://www.socialsecurity.gov/pubs/10043.html

Mississippi Division of Medicaid (March 1, 2007)

Medicaid Eligibility Guide-Mississippi, Can I Qualify for Medicaid? Retrieved on February 1, 2008

http://www.dom.state.ms.us/Eligibility/QualifyingForMedicaid72005.pdf

Picture of President Johnson signing the Medicare program into law,

July 30, 1965…courtesy LBJ Presidential Library

http://www.ssa.gov/history/lbjsm.html

Medicare Survival Guide Advanced®, May 2018; King, Toni

Most of the knowledge about Medicare for this guide comes from my experience with training and certification classes about the Medicare and Health Insurance industry.

About the Author

Toni King has more than 20 years of experience as a top sales leader of Medicare plans. When Toni saw the recurring theme of confusion as it relates to understanding the rules of Medicare for choosing a plan that would best suit the needs of each individual client, she was inspired to write her first book, The Medicare Survival Guide®

Toni King is an accomplished Medicare advocate, author, radio talk show personality having both hosted and been a guest of numerous programs, a newspaper columnist and public speaker. She also hosts and presents "Confused About Medicare" workshops to the public throughout the United States, helping thousands navigate what so many consider to be the "Medicare maze."